THE ELECTRIC GUITAR

Its History
and Construction
by
Donald Brosnac

Panjandrum Press

1975 San Francisco

Distributed to the music trade by:
MUSIC SALES CORPORATION
33 West 60 Street   New York 10023

Fret spacings © Rickenbacker 1974, used by permission.

Library of Congress Cataloging in Publication Data

Brosnac, Donald, 1947-

The Electric Guitar, Its History and Construction.

   1. Guitar—History. 2. Guitar—Construction.

I. Title.

ML1015.G9B76   787'.61   75-9539

ISBN 0-915572-00-1

First Printing: June 1975
Second Printing: September 1975

Also by the same author:
*The Steel String Guitar: Its History
& Construction* (Panjandrum Press, 1973)

PANJANDRUM PRESS
99 Sanchez St., San Francisco, California 94114

Manufactured in the United States of America

Acknowledgments

I WOULD like to thank the following persons for the generous amount of information and time they granted me, for without their help this book would not have been possible:

Vince Basse—*Fender*
Richard Brosnac
Carl Countryman—*C. Countryman & Associates*
Lester Davidson—*Martin*
Rudy Dopyera—*Original Musical Instrument Co.*
George Falaney—*Harmony*
Walter Fuller—*Gibson*
Eric Gaer—*Acoustic*
Larry Goldstein—*Harmony*
Doug Green—*Country Music Hall of Fame,
        Nashville, Tennessee*
John Hall—*Rickenbacker*
Jerry Hogerson—*Altec*
Hideo Kamimoto—*builder and repairman,
        Oakland, California*
"Doc" Kaufman—*K & F*
Ken Killman—*Gibson*
Duke Kramer—*Gretsch*
Robb Lawrence-*guitar historian*
Arnie Lazarus—*Frap*
Jim Lehmann—*Guitar Resurrection*
Neil Lilien—*Guild*
George Lockwood—*Guild*
Mike Longworth—*Martin*
Seth Lover—*Gibson and Fender* (retired)
Wilbur Marker—*Gibson* (retired)
J. D. Massa—*Ampeg*
Ted McCarty—*Bigsby* (formerly of Gibson)
Pete Mundy—*Alembic*
John Quarterman—*Orig. Musical Instrument Co.*
James Rickard—*Ovation*
Horace Rowe—*Rowe*
Harmon Satterlee—*builder and repairman, San
        Francisco, California*
Fred Tavares—*Fender*
Don Thompson—*Martin*
Rick Turner—*Alembic*
Ed Woznike—*Harmony*

Information about photographs:

The guitars on the cover (from left to right) are: A National solid-body guitar, circa 1936; an Epiphone "Zephyr Deluxe Regent", circa 1949; and a Bigsby-Travis solid-body, 1947.

Photo on the back cover shows one step in the process of constructing a hollow body guitar.

All photographs were taken by Donald Brosnac except the Gretsch White Falcon — courtesy of Gretsch, the Harmony Guitars—courtesy of Harmony, the Guild Artist Award—courtesy of Guild, the Rickenbacker 360—courtesy of Rickenbacker, and the F.R.A.P. pick-up—courtesy of F.R.A.P. The photo of the B. C. Rich Seagull was supplied by L. D. Heater, and the photo of the Framus Nashville Standard was supplied by Framus.

Contents

Dedication

This book is dedicated to those who use music as a vehicle for sharing honest revelations of weakness and strength.

Introduction

THIS BOOK is written for all persons who enjoy the guitar. The *electric* guitar presents an attraction to a wide variety of people—from musicians playing entertaining music and doing sound experimentation, to those interested in woodworking, craftsmanship or electronics, and finally to those persons who support the music industry through their patronization and appreciation.

The electric guitar is a fascinating instrument to study, especially since so many developments have occurred in a short span of time. Perhaps no other instrument can boast such a mercurial rise to prominence—from birth to its dominance in contemporary music in just thirty years. Thousands of musicians throughout the world find the electric guitar a mode of self-expression, social enjoyment, and for many, a lucrative profession. From its early uses with country music to its present use in nearly all forms of music, the electric guitar expresses much of the powerful intensity of modern day life.

The development of this extraordinary instrument is traced from early scientific experiments and home-made devices down to present state-of-the-art electronic wizardry. In over thirty outstanding, rare and historical examples, the evolution of the electronic guitar is depicted in photographs and text.

The guitar's structural elements—the body, mechanical devices, and electronic components — are taken apart and explained as to why they are designed as they are and how they work. The reader also will learn which types of strings to use and how to extend their life, why his guitar can be hard to tune, and how it can be made easier to play. The mysterious realm of guitar electronics is revealed in the examination of the components made by all the major guitar-making companies. Amplifiers, speakers and sound embellishment devices are examined as they relate to the needs of the electric guitar player.

Lastly, but surely not the least, in photographs, schematic drawings and text, the construction of two of the most popular electric guitars—the hollow body and solid body electric guitars—is presented step-by-step for those persons desiring to make their own guitar.

Professional musicians, instrument builders, as well as those persons with a casual interest in the guitar, will find in this book a wealth of information not presented before.

It would give me pleasure to be able to state that I have presented a complete book on the electric guitar; but, as so often happens, the gathering of information on any subject is at the same time a process of discovering just how immense the subject is. Although I have tried to include as much information as possible, to have enlarged on the present book would have served only to confuse, not to communicate. As for some guitars I have excluded, I would recommend such books as Mike Longworth's on Martin guitars and the Gibson Company's forthcoming book on its history. And now, on to the electric guitar!

Donald Brosnac
Bolinas, California 1975

Origin of the Electric Guitar

THOUGH THE KNOWLEDGE of the first individual to coax an electrically amplified sound out of a guitar is lost in a Sargasso Sea of ingenious but ineffective ideas, there does remain a voluminous amount of information regarding the earliest electric guitars that did work.

In the shadowy realm of fragmentary historical records, the most often repeated tale is of a foreigner (sometimes Austrian, Australian or English) who made an electric guitar in the 1920's. This elusive gentleman has not left anything more than the recollection: ". . . yes, there was someone, an Englishman, I think . . . in the twenties . . . a magnetic pick-up, I believe . . ." in the memories of those persons intimately involved with the electric guitar's birth. Though there is much hearsay, I have endeavored to write only that which can be substantially documented.

* * *

The birth and development of the electric guitar and its related electronics, offers an insight into the evolution of artistic expression and cultural values of the U.S., as well as other areas of the world. This maturation of the electric guitar, however, was preceded by innovations with acoustic guitars.

The soft sound of the classic guitar evolved to the louder, brasher steel-strung flat and arched top guitars of the twenties and thirties. The invention of a metal resonator guitar—the Dobro and National—produced a more piercing sound. Even with Lloyd Loar's and Guy Hart's creation, the L-5, (its sound is referred to as "cutting power"), more was needed.

Guitarists played into mikes, or put mikes on or in guitars. Feedback and unwanted noise was a continuing problem. A method was needed that could make loud music solely from the guitar's strings. As music became more professional, musicians' styles expanded. The desire to play quickly over the complete fret length led to the development of the neck being joined to the body at the 14th fret instead of the 12th like a classical guitar. This allowed for easier playing. But still more was needed. Gibson made the L-5 Premier in the thirties with a cut-away to facilitate fingering, and an arched fretboard to help further. Some modern electrics virtually join neck and body at the last fret.

* * *

The earliest substantiated electric pick-up for a guitar is the electrostatic device made by Lloyd Loar in about 1923. Walter Fuller of Gibson told me this device had two diaphragms with charged particles that were separated by insulation material. The diaphragms were copper discs about the size of a half dollar. An electric current was induced in these discs and leads were taken off with a capacitor in series to the grid of the amp used. This assembly had a very high impedance, about 1 Meg Ohm. The unit was encased in bakelite, but it was never possible to seal against humidity, making it noisy and less sensitive.

Carl Countryman, the makers of a sophisticated phase-shifter, currently makes an electrostatic capacitance pick-up for pianos. This type of pick-up is now technically possible with integrated circuits. Capacitance pick-ups cannot tolerate any length of cabling between the transducer and the necessary pre-amps. In 1923, before solid state electronics, this would have meant a tube amp inside a guitar.

* * *

In 1924, Lloyd Loar left Gibson to form his own company to manufacture electric instruments. It was about this time that he made an electric double bass. However, satisfactory consumer response and technical devolopment of electric instruments did not occur for another ten years. In 1928, the Amperite Company, in conjunction with Benjamin Messner, made a contact microphone that was used on guitars.

* * *

In the late twenties and early thirties, inventive musicians adapted phonograph cartridges for guitar pick-up use. Alvino Rey and Les Paul are two of the musicians who have had a hand in this area of experimentation. Les Paul continued with his electric guitar experiments which in time culminated in the Gibson-Les Paul guitars.

Mr. De Armond was a musician who developed a pickup for "F" hole guitars in about 1931. He worked with Horace Rowe and together they made the Rowe-De Armond pick-up, style FH-C. The Rowe Company was one of the first suppliers of pick-ups to guitar makers. As far as I'm concerned, not enough credit is given to the Rowe Company for the development of the electric guitar.

Fred Tavares, who invented the Stratocaster, told me that in 1932 he made an electric guitar by using an RCA phonograph pick-up adapted for use on his guitar.

* * *

George Beauchamp and Paul Barth made an electric guitar in 1931. Beauchamp's guitar had a pick-up that was made with a coil surrounded by horseshoe magnets. These magnets were tungsten steel that had been subjected to an intense prolonged electric current (thanks to the power company next door) to make them magnetic. Since Western Electric made amps and held most of the patents, the Rickenbacker Company, for which Beauchamp worked, arranged for a co-use of patents between the companies. The production model Hawaiian guitar had a one-piece aluminum body with a hollow neck. The patent, No. 2,089,171, was not obtained until August 10, 1937.

In 1932, the Dopyera Brothers (DOBRO) made a few of their resonator guitars with an electric pick-up in conjunction with guitarist Art Simpson. This guitar's pick-up had high impedance and was made with a bar magnet wound with copper wire. It is thought to be the first manufactured electric Spanish guitar. The Gibson Company started to make electric steel guitars and Electric Spanish guitars in the '30's. The E.S. series continues to the present. During this time John Moore joined

Gibson, and together they developed the Gibson Electraharp. This was the first pedal steel.

Lyon and Healy was the firm that manufactured the amplifiers that Gibson used with its first electric guitar. This Hawaiian guitar was shaped similar to a Rickenbacker BD-6 and had a cast aluminum body like the earlier "frying pan." Though information is scarce, it is believed that this electric steel guitar was first made in 1935. The Gibson Co. made electric Hawaiian guitars (EH-150), electric Spanish guitars (ES-150), and electric tenor banjos (ETB-150) in the late thirties, all with similar wire wound bar magnet pick-ups.

* * *

In 1947, Paul Bigsby and Merle Travis worked together in Downey, California to develop the first solid body electric guitar to be used conventionally, that is, not a Hawaiian guitar. It is shaped like a Spanish guitar and fretted with fingers. It is similar in shape to a Les Paul. It has an alnico bar magnet high impedance pick-up. Ted McCarty who supplied me information believes it is made of maple.

Leo Fender and Doc Kaufman worked together to produce the K and F electric steel guitar in 1944. In 1946 Kaufman left. In 1948 Leo Fender with George Fullerton built the first solid wood-bodied electric guitar to achieve economic and musical success. Mr. Fender began developing this guitar himself in 1947. This guitar was the Broadcaster. It is similar to the Bigsby-Travis guitar. Very soon the name was changed to Telecaster, since Gretsch had used that name—Broadcaster—for the drums and banjos they made. A later development of the K and F guitar made by Fender had many of the same features, but had a solid pearloid plastic body.

In order to cope with the problem of acoustic feedback (the guitar body vibrating from amplifier speaker sound) in electric Spanish guitars, the fifties saw the creation of guitars with less body depth. These thin body guitars are less prone to feedback.

In 1954, Fred Tavares worked with Fender to invent the Stratocaster, which is probably the most popular electric guitar. And in the mid-fifties Rickenbacker came out with a guitar that had a built-in pre-amp. In order to fit it inside, hearing-aid tubes were used.

About 1956, another of the big patented inventions was made. Seth Lover and Ted McCarty invented the humbucking pick-up while working for Gibson. This pick-up reproduced less hum, resulting from placing two coils next to each other and wiring parallel with opposite magnetic polarities. In 1973, the patent ran out and nearly all guitar companies make one now. The humbucking is not the ultimate pick-up though. Much work is being done presently to develop pick-ups of strong response that are of high fidelity. Pick-ups with different kinds of magnetic cores are being tested, and some may even be on the market by now.

Several years ago, the quest of sound reproduction was in the direction of clear, faithful sound. At present, there is demand for super powerful pick-ups that can overdrive an amp to produce distortion and many varieties of sound. How long this will continue, I don't know. The Gibson Super Humbucking with ceramic magnets encapsulated in epoxy was made for this demand. This pick-up was made by Bill Lawrence and Walter Fuller.

In the late sixties the Gibson Co. and Les Paul developed the Les Paul Recording guitar. A high and low impedance switch allows the guitar to be either low impedance for direct injection into a recording studio board or normal high impedance performing amps for concert use.

Work is being done on pick-ups that are variable in impedance and have separate controls for picking-up each string.

*   *   *

In the preceding I have concentrated on the magnetic pick-up. Piezo-electric transducers have been around for a long time, but the technology required to produce acceptable sound is recent. There has not been very much enthusiasm for these devices in the past, but now with the very successful Ovation acoustic/electric guitars, many guitar companies are interested.

A piezo-electric transducer contains a type of natural crystal or manufactured ceramic material that will generate an electro-mechanical force when it is subject to mechanical stress. Transducer simply means a device that is activated by power from one system and supplies power in a different form to another system. When a string is vibrating back and forth, it is causing changing pressures (mechanical stress) on the piezo-electric transducer. It works by changes of pressure, not electromagnetic fields. Any type of strings can be used. Some of the natural crystals that can be used are rochelle salts, tourmaline, quartz, and even, though to a much lesser extent, cane sugar crystals. As early as 1880,

Pierre and Jacques Curie discovered that some crystals when compressed in particular directions showed positive and negative charges on parts of their surfaces. (1)

There are two basic types of piezo-electric elements. One type works by applied direct pressure, the other works when put under a bending pressure. The former requires more force to drive. The Rowe Company makes a pick-up with a Lead Zirconate Titante crystal bonded to an acoustic diaphragm. This device is very efficient and does not require a pre-amp to boost its signal like most other piezo pick-ups.

Gibson has made a pick-up used on one of their guitars, model C100E, that used a bending crystal. This pick-up had a silver plate pressure-formed coating on each side with leads from opposite sides of the crystal. There was a separate element for each string. It was made from 1964 to 1967. Other popular pick-ups are Barcus Berry and F.R.A.P. (flat response audio pick-up). I know someone who uses a Barcus Berry on their cello. The F.R.A.P. pick-up is the invention of Arnie Lazurus. He developed it in 1969 and states that it gets a virtually flat response (faithful sound reproduction) from 5 cycles per second to 100,000 cycles per second. That's a range from far below human hearing to far above. This unit, that requires four batteries for a portable pre-amp, is probably the most advanced piezo pick-up made.

*   *   *

The Barcus-Berry pick-up is the creation of Les Barcus and John Berry of Long Beach, California. The "Hot Dot" pick-up is a recent Barcus-Berry concept. Two dot-like piezo elements inserted into a guitar bridge (a nodal area) receive acoustic string energy and cancel finger noise.

The Ovation acoustic/electric guitars are the ones that showed what could be done. The pick-up uses separate elements under each string with a pre-amp built into the guitar with a volume knob on the outside "Lyrachord" bowl. The sound reproduction of these guitars is very accurate.

In the foregoing, I have not gone into the parts of magnetic pick-ups and how they work, while I have in respect to piezo-electric units. This will be covered in a following chapter.

(1) Walter G. Cady, *Piezoelectricity* (McGraw-Hill, N.Y., 1946), p. 2.

There are numerous inventions in pick-ups that would be confusing to try to list in chronological order with the major developments mentioned. These other developments are important because they may be used in different forms to make new pick-ups. The Rowe Co. has patented a system of bonding threads to pole magnets which in turn are screwed into a plastic bobbin on which the copper wire is wound. This allows one to adjust a magnet up or down to set pick-up strength of each string. The Rowe Company made a demonstration model that had a separate pick-up for each string and each of these was fed to a separate amp channel so that each could be precisely controlled.

Ray Butts worked with Chet Atkins to develop the Gretsch Filtertron pick-up. The Filtertron has a double row of magnets with a separate coil for picking-up each string. Gretsch pioneered stereo guitars with a pick-up split in half. Three bass strings had their own lead and the three treble strings had theirs.

In about 1968 or 1969, the Gretsch Company made a guitar—the "Rally"—with a pre-amp. The Roc II likewise has solid state internal electronics. The HI-A Company makes a low impedance, high output pick-up that has separate outputs for each string. The pick-ups are encapsulated in epoxy resin. Gretsch makes their Supertron I with laminated iron cores which support the dual coils and extend to the magnet used in common. It is felt the laminated iron gives an edge to the sound. The Supertron II looks similar but has solid iron cores (bars).

Alembic makes some advanced electronic circuits, which are covered in the chapters, "Historically Significant Guitars" and "Electric Guitar Pick-ups.

The evolution of the acoustic guitar travels at the pace of craftspersons handworking wood and patiently listening to sound. The evolution of the electric guitar occurs at the speed of developments in the scientific/industrial electronics industry. The lag between developments in one branch of electronics and when those developments are used by the music industry is closing. One guitar in particular, the Rickenbacker 360, is a good example of the current rapid evolution. This guitar, brought out in about 1960, is now undergoing so many changes that it is hard to write about. A new two-octave neck and continual pick-up changes are currently a mark of this guitar.

Now, is anyone ready to make a laser beam pick-up?

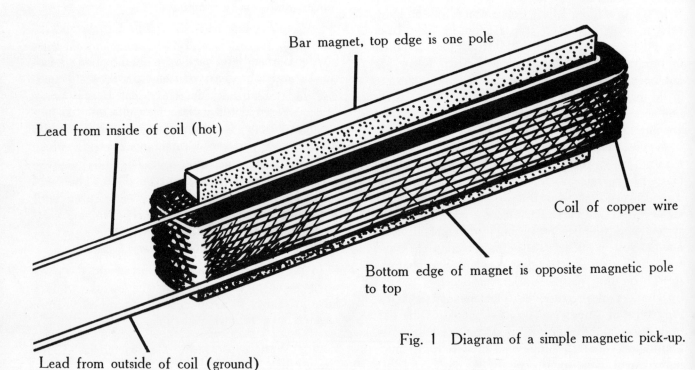

Bar magnet, top edge is one pole

Lead from inside of coil (hot)

Coil of copper wire

Bottom edge of magnet is opposite magnetic pole to top

Lead from outside of coil (ground)

Fig. 1 Diagram of a simple magnetic pick-up.

Historically Significant Guitars

GIBSON—'C' 1900
FIG. 2

THIS GUITAR was made by Orville Gibson himself. Its unique features include: Sides that are not bent, but rather, cut out in shape from a large block of walnut; an arched Norwegian spruce sound-board; a one-piece carved walnut back; banjo-like machines; and intricate tortoise shell, abalone and pearl inlay. In addition, it has a hollow neck, a feature on many of Gibson's instruments, which adds sound chamber volume. The neck is correspondingly fat. This guitar has a very full and balanced sound. Although acoustic, it demonstrates admirably the evolution that steel strung guitars have undergone.

Photographed at the Gibson Company.

FIG. 3

GIBSON—'L-5' 1924
FIG. 4

THE L-5 IS THE CREATION of Lloyd Loar and Guy Hart. The instrument is a development from Orville's guitars of 1900. His guitars had carved tops and backs, but still conformed to a basic guitar format. The "L" guitars made by the Gibson Company were more strongly based on violins; some advertisements proclaimed that Gibson guitars used the knowledge of Stradivarius. The guitars had a separate bridge and string anchor, and violin-shaped carved arched maple back and spruce top. The "F" holes were vital in shaping the instrument's brilliant and piercing sound. These guitars were one of the first to have fourteen frets of the fingerboard/neck clear of the body. The one shown is not totally an original since it has had some parts replaced: The fretboard is mid-forties, the tailpiece is from another L-5, and the pick-guard has been lost.

Photographed at Lundberg's Music Store, Berkeley, California.

NATIONAL
—'Tri-plate' 1926
FIG. 5

SHOWN HERE ARE A National tri-plate resonator guitar and a National single resonator. The National, made of a nickle and silver alloy, was hand-hammered to shape on cast iron forming molds.

The resonator guitar was developed by the Dopyera brothers primarily because of musicians' need for instruments of greater volume. It is best known as being used for slide (Hawaiian) playing.

The National was photographed at the Original Musical Instrument Company in Long Beach, California.

NATIONAL
—'Duolian' c. 1928

FIG. 6

THIS NATIONAL metal body guitar is similar to the National Tri-Plate, but has only a single plate (resonator cone). Compare it to the 1932 Dobro electric.

Photographed at the Nashville Hall of Fame and Museum.

RICKENBACKER
—'Prototype Electric' 1931
FIG. 7

THE A-22 and A-25 "frying pan guitars" were the first commercially produced electric guitars. The numbers 22 and 25 refer to scale length. Shown is the first Rickenbacker guitar—a wooden-bodied prototype. The all aluminum guitar is the production model. In addition to the aluminum model, another one was made with a solid bakelite body.

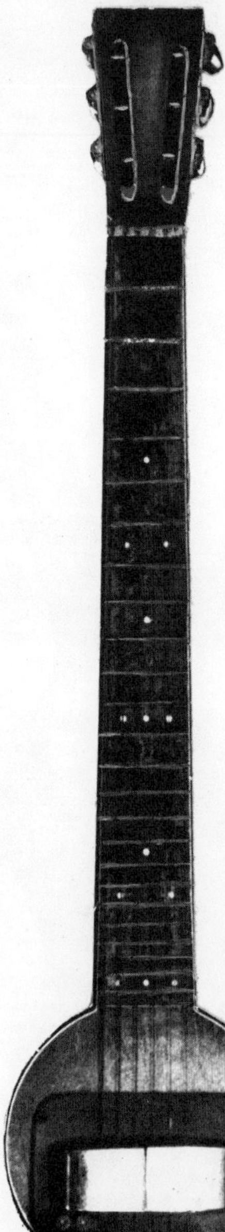

The prototype was photographed at the Rickenbacker Company, the aluminum model at the Fender Company,

RICKENBACKER ☞
—'Frying Pan' 1931
FIG. 8

DOBRO—electric 1932
FIG. 9

IN 1932, Dobro electrics were made with a bar magnet pick-up installed in conjunction with the resonator and cover plate. This very early electric suffered from technical difficulties, and the later solid cast aluminum Dobro and National guitars are the descendants of these prototypes. The guitar shown is a contemporary acoustic Dobro, very much like the 1932 electrified version.

Photographed at the Fifth String, San Francisco

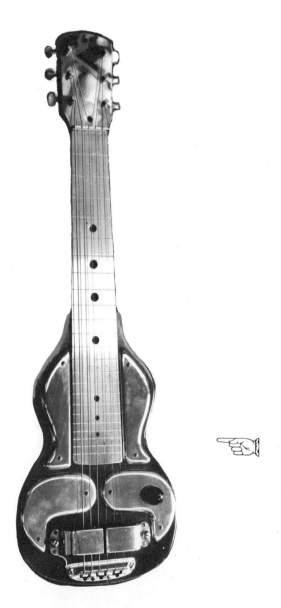

RICKENBACKER
'BD-6' 1935
Figs. 10 11 & 12

THIS GUITAR was brought out in 1935. The body is two-piece bakelite and was also known as the Electro. There is a BD-6 in the Nashville Hall of Fame Museum that was Jerry Bird's first professional instrument. Also shown is a two piece mahogany bodied guitar believed to be a prototype.

Photographed at Kamimoto Strings, Oakland.

Photographed at George Peacock's Guitar Shop, San Francisco.

FIG. 11

FIG. 12

GIBSON
—'ES-150' c. 1935

FIG. 13

THIS IS the Gibson Company's earliest production electric Spanish guitar. Previously, like many other companies, Gibson had also made electric Hawaiian guitars. The ES-150 was about the same size as an L-5 and had one magnetic pick-up. Shown here is an ES-125 (c. 1950) which is retouched to resemble an ES-150. The ES-150 had more binding, and a different pick-up and fretboard than the ES-125.

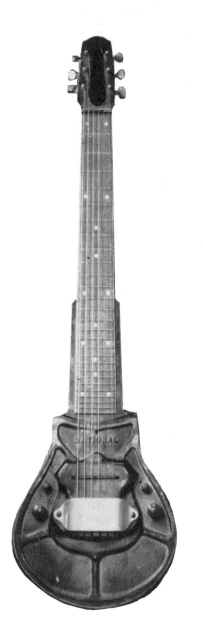

NATIONAL
—solidbody c. 1936
FIG. 14

THIS MODEL is one of the strangest looking electric guitars ever made. Made by the same company that made resonator guitars, this instrument has a one-piece, cast aluminum body and a wooden fretboard. During this same period of time, the Dobro Company was making both solid body aluminum and hardwood body Hawaiian guitars. In addition, both National and Dobro made an arched top "F" hole guitar with a single bar magnet pick-up.

Photographed at The Guitar Center, San Francisco.

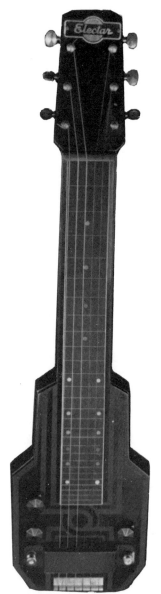

EPIPHONE
—'Electar' c. late 1930's or early 1940's
FIG. 15

THIS HAWAIIAN guitar is an example of Epiphone's early electric guitars. It's a real rare bird.

Photographed at Prune Music, Mill Valley.

K & F
—Hawaiian 1944
FIG. 16

THIS INSTRUMENT WAS MADE by the K and F Radio and Television Supply Company from a block of maple. Fashioned almost entirely on a drill press, it has a trochoidal magnetic pick-up. The scale is twenty-two and ⅝ inches in length; the fret positions were painted on. The initials "K" and "F" actually stood for Doc Kaufman and Leo Fender. In 1946, Doc left K and F, and Leo started the Fender Musical Instrument Company.

Photographed at the Fender Company.

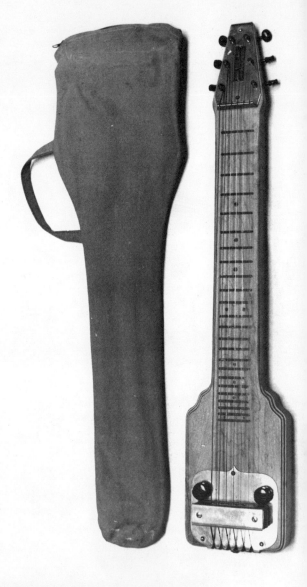

FIG. 17

BIGSBY & TRAVIS
—solidbody 1947
Figs. 18 & 19

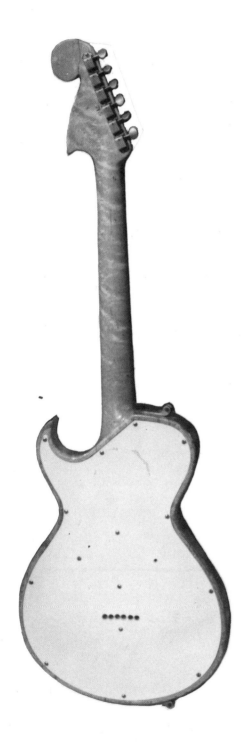

THIS IS THE first "modern" electric. The body is maple with the insides carved out for the electronic components. There is a plexiglass plate that covers the back and the interior compartment. The guitar has a fairly straight neck and its shape, along with the rosewood fretboard, allows it to fit very comfortably into the hands. It is interesting to compare this guitar — which was made and played in Downey, Calif. — to Fender guitars which are made in nearby Fullerton.

Photographed at the Nashville Hall of Fame and Museum.

FENDER
—'Broadcaster' 1948
FIG. 20

THIS WAS invented by Leo Fender and is one of the first solid bodies. Since Gretsch had first used the name Broadcaster, Fender changed the name to Telecaster in 1950. With its two single coil pick-ups, the guitar remains much the same as it was in 1948. The only changes are minor—a different pick-guard and neck reinforcement. The Blond model is ash; painted versions are alder.

Photographed at Guitar Resurrection, Austin Texas.

EPIPHONE
—'Zephyr Deluxe Regent' c. 1949
FIG. 21

THE ORIGINAL Epiphone Company, no longer in business, was founded by Epi A. Stathopoulo. In 1958, the Gibson Company bought it out.

This guitar is an old hollow body electric. The top and back are arched, laminated maple, and the back has a bird's-eye maple grain. The neck consists of pieces of maple, walnut and mahogany laminated lengthwise, and joins the body at the 14th fret, with twenty frets total. The fretboard, bound in dark and light binding, has a 25½ inch scale. Gold finish pick-ups are mounted in yellow plastic. The body is 3⅜ in. deep, 17⅜ in. wide, and 20¾ in. long; overall length is 41½ in. Although this guitar possesses no startling electronic innovations, it is quite a show of design and craftsmanship.

Photographed at the Rowe Company.

GRETSCH
—'Synchromatic' c. 1949
FIG. 22

THIS GUITAR has stylish teardrop-shaped sound-holes. The original pick-ups have been replaced and more modern Gretsch pick-ups mounted on rubber washers have been installed. The bridge is believed to have been replaced also.

Photographed at George Peacock's Guitar Shop, San Francisco.

"chromatic" tailpiece

GIBSON
—'Les Paul' 1952
FIG. 23

THE FIRST Gibson Les Paul was made in 1952, so this 1954 version pictured here is one of the first. Les Paul, who had worked with Gibson to manufacture this model, had taken an acoustic guitar, cut it in half and then filled the body with shaped wood to make it solid. This guitar, being an early model, does not have the more recent humbucking pick-ups. The body itself is a solid piece of mahogany with a solid ½ in. exterior carved piece of maple laminated to it to form a top. There are many versions of Les Paul guitars made by Gibson at present.

Photographed at Guitar Resurrection, Austin Texas.

GRETSCH
'White Falcon' 1953
FIG. 24

THE GRETSCH COMPANY, founded by Fred Gretsch in 1883, was at first primarily engaged in the manufacture of drums and banjos, but later diversified into other instruments. Gretsch is quite well known for its line of guitars designed by Chet Atkins who has worked with company engineers to develop many hollow-body electric guitars. Duke Kramer of Gretsch has told me that solid carved wood is not an asset to hollow-body electrics: For this reason, their hollow-bodies have laminated arched tops and backs. This laminated wood is not a cheap core with pretty veneers, but rather three pieces of maple joined together with opposing grain directions. The White Falcon, with a bridge that floats over the body, is the finest of all Gretsch guitars. Gretsch also makes a seven-string Van Eps guitar on special order.

FENDER
—'Stratocaster' 1954
FIG. 25

THE STRATOCASTER was developed in 1954 by Fred Tavares. It has three staggered-height alnico pole magnet single coil pick-ups, which are similar to those of a Tele. The neck is maple, having twenty-one frets and optional tremelo. Natural and walnut finish Fender guitars are made of ash; painted ones of alder. Fender beginners' guitars are made of poplar. Finishes are a combination of lacquers and polyesters—the guitar shown has a sunburst finish. Jimi Hendrix was probably the most famous player of this guitar.

Photographed at The Guitar Center, this guitar is a 1974 model.

THIS WAS BUILT for Joe Maphis by Semie Mosley, founder of the Mosrite Company. The guitar has a hollowed out inside and thus is not as heavy as it appears. One neck is a standard six string guitar neck, and the other, though it too uses six strings, is tuned an octave higher.

Double neck electric guitars are quite common. Variations include a standard six string guitar and standard four string bass, a six and a twelve-string guitar, and fretted four string bass and non-fretted bass. The necks of double neck guitars often diverge at an angle from the body. This is thought to facilitate playing. Parallel necks are becoming more common though.

Photographed at the Nashville Hall of Fame and Museum.

MOSRITE
—'Joe Maphis' 1954
FIG. 26

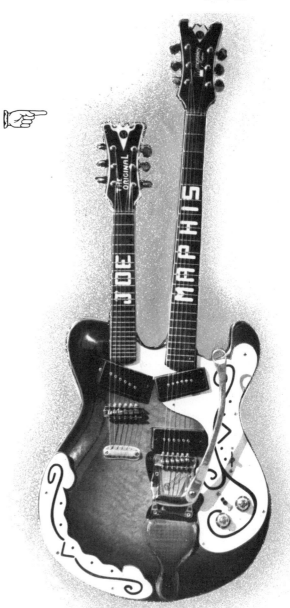

GUILD
—'Artist Award'
c. 1955
FIG. 27

IN REGARD TO the electric guitar's history, the instrument shown here is of vital importance. It is like one of the first electric guitars made, the guitar that used the first pick-up made in 1932 by Mr. De Armond and Mr. Rowe. The Guild Company presently makes this guitar, with an arched style top, as their top of the line model. Without overlooking the importance of inlays and other embellishments, much work was done to develop its distinctive brightness and balance of tone. This guitar first came out as the Johnny Smith Award Model and was changed in name to the Artist Award Model two or three years later.

GIBSON

—'Flying V' c. 1958

FIG. 28

THIS RADICALLY shaped solid body (Korina mahogany) was first made in late 1958. The body shape certainly demonstrates that an electric guitar need not look like a guitar! This particular Flying V has been restored to mint condition, with a new clear finish. The hardware is gold-plated, and the fretboard is rosewood.

Photographed at Guitar Resurrection, Austin Texas.

HARMONY

—'H-655' 1958

FIG. 29

THIS IS an acoustic/electric guitar. If the control knobs were black and mounted on the pickguard, many people wouldn't be able to tell this instrument was electric. One unique feature is that the pick-up is mounted *under* the end of the fretboard with only the pole adjustment screws showing. The instrument, of course, has its own distinctive sound. Compare it with the photo of the Martin D-28E: Because of the two pick-ups on that guitar, the top had to have heavier bracing, thereby reducing acoustic sound. The D-28E pick-ups also add a terrific amount of dead weight to the soundboard.

The predecessor of the H-655, the H-40 was introduced in 1953. This guitar had the same electronics but was not as refined in regard to finish.

MARTIN
—'D-28E' 1959
FIG. 31

THIS GUITAR is a rare bird. The magnetic pickups are similar to the ones on the Martin GT-75. The guitar is basically a D-28 with the addition of two magnetic pick-ups. Since I have not been able to find an intact D-28E, I spliced two photographs together (this D-28E had no neck).

Besides the D-28E and GT-75, Martin has made 6 other electric models. The 00-18E, GT-70 and the F-50 (an arched-top electric) are some of the other Martin electrics.

GRETSCH
—'Tennessean' c. 1958
FIG. 30

THIS GUITAR (Serial #67786) at first glance appears to be an orthodox "F" hole hollow body, but closer examination reveals that the "F" holes are merely painted on! Ordinary hollow body guitars are prone to feedback problems, since the body picks up amplified sound vibrations. Some musicians have stuffed their guitars with cloth to absorb such vibrations. Thus, for a short time, Gretsch made some of their hollow body guitars without sound holes to resist this feedback. Besides looking quite tasteful, the painted "F" holes convey the idea that the guitar is hollow.

Photographed at Guitar Resurrection, Austin Texas.

GUILD
—'X-350' c. late 1950's
FIG. 32

THIS IS ONE of the earliest Guild guitars. Many Epiphone craftsmen went to work for Guild when Epiphone went out of business. The influence of these talented people is shown in this maple back, side and top "F" hole guitar. This guitar has three single coil pick-ups. There are six push buttons that control the selection of pick-ups:

    1—"B" bass pick-up
    2—"M" middle pick-up
    3—"T" treble pick-up
    4—"MB"   5—"TB"   6—"TM".

Photographed at Guitar Resurrection, Austin Texas.

RICKENBACKER
—'360' c. 1960
FIG. 33

This thin-bodied guitar has several unique features and optional slanted frets. First all the frets are slanted eight degrees to facilitate fast fingering. Musicians I have spoken to said that the sloping frets feel awkward at first, but once gotten used to, they prove to be very fast. Second, the guitar has outputs for both monaural and stereo sound. Third, the semi-acoustic body has one sound hole quite removed from an "F" configuration.

It is fitting to note here that many standard features of other electric guitars were developed by Rickenbacker. Reasons for this include the fact that Rickenbacker has made parts for other companies, and moreover, ex-Rickenbacker employees have started their own companies, drawing on their past experience. This guitar has a 24-fret (two octave) neck.

MARTIN
—'GT-75' 1965
FIG. 34

MOST PEOPLE aren't aware that the Martin Company has made electric guitars. About 750 of the GT-75 (pictured here) were made between 1965 and 1967. Mike Longworth has informed me that "the design was a cooperative effort, and no one person was responsible. In the last analysis, Mr. C. F. Martin III had the final say regarding such designs. The pick-ups used were MA-5 type made by Rowe . . ."

This hollow body guitar is painted maroon and has a white body and fretboard binding. It is also equipped with an adjustable truss rod instead of the usual Martin non-adjustable rod.

Photographed at Kamimoto Strings, Oakland.

FENDER – 12-string 1965
FIG. 35

THIS PARTICULAR guitar is no longer made. It is similar to other solid body Fender guitars, and is included to show that 12-string electric guitars *are* possible. It is no longer made because there was not sufficient demand for it.

AMPEG
—'Dan Armstrong' 1969
FIG. 36

THIS GUITAR, designed by Dan Armstrong, has a clear plastic body and Dan Armstrong pick-ups. Armstrong instruments were first made in 1969, but owing to too little popularity, are no longer produced. I have included this example to show the range of materials that can be used in constructing electric guitars. Dan now makes guitars and basses in England with a single pick-up that slides to any position between the end of fretboard and bridge. Ampeg currently makes a solid-body guitar that is made of a multitude of thin pieces of wood laminated together.

Photographed at The Guitar Center, San Francisco.

OVATION
'Electric Country Artist' 1971
FIG. 37

OVATION HAS BOTH steel and nylon strung guitars with piezo-electric pick-ups mounted in the bridge. Separate pick-ups for each string are fed into an FET pre-amp inside the guitar. The pre-amp is powered by a nine volt battery, and a volume knob is outside on the upper bout. The main sound picked up is that of the vibrating strings. The sound of the guitar being rubbed against the player or the sound of fingers tapping the body will not be heard. This is very important since contact mics amplify all the sound from the guitar.

Photographed at the Ovation Company.

OVATION
—'Deacon' 1972
FIG. 38

SINCE OVATION'S earliest days, James Rickard, the Engineering and Quality Control Manager, has worked on the company's instrument development program. He personally designed the Piezo electric pick-up for the acoustic electric guitar, and also the solid body "Breadwinner-Deacon" guitars. The electronics of the solid body include a printed circuit that provides for constant level sound when the tone controls are used to cut the treble or bass frequencies. The tone controls involve mainly capacitors, chokes (coils), and transistors. The circuit provides uniform sound when either pick-up is used, even when they are engaged out-of-phase (which normally results in a substantial drop in volume).

Photographed at the Ovation Company.

IT'S INTERESTING to notice the development of electric guitars from the Rickenbacker "frying pan" through various solid and hollow body wooden models to this modern aluminum instrument. It is machined from two solid blocks for the body and the slim neck, rather than its being created from formed, sheet aluminum. The neck is very thin and hence, easy to reach around. The guitar is equipped with humbucking pick-ups and Schaller tuning machines. It weighs approximately 8¼ lbs.

Photographed at The Guitar Center, San Francisco.

VELENO
—'Original' 1972
FIG. 39

GIBSON
—'Howard Roberts'
C. 1973   FIG. 40

IT IS INTRIGUING to compare this body shape to the Orville Gibson Style "C" guitar shown earlier in this section. The tops are both arched and have similar soundholes. Gibson has made more guitars styled after the tastes of prominent artists than any other company. Howard Roberts worked with Gibson to construct a guitar with the sound, feel and appearance he desired; the pick-up and controls were developed specifically for this guitar. Just as most Gibson electrics have humbucking pick-ups, many of them have pick-ups with features designed for an individual guitar.

From a purely acoustic standpoint, the sound of this laminated wood guitar is difficult to judge, since it is meant for electric use. Another interesting comparison is between the oval soundhole tone and the tone of an "F" hole guitar of similar body size. The original Howard Roberts guitar was made by Epiphone.

Photographed at The Guitar Center, San Francisco.

HARMONY
—'H-684' 1974
FIG. 41

THIS SINGLE "F" hole guitar is unique in that the volume and tone controls for each pick-up are sliding levers, instead of conventional rotating knobs. Since the finish has negligible effect in regard to sound, Harmony graces this guitar—along with others it manufactures—with the image of beautiful rosewood painted on the body.

The predecessor of the H-684 was the H-82 made in 1968. This guitar pioneered linear variable resistors.

ALEMBIC—1974
FIG. 42

THIS SMALL California company is doing some of the most advanced electronics work in the world. Alembic guitars and basses are acclaimed for their sound, a result of their advanced electronic systems. Both bass and guitar have high-strength, low-impedance pick-ups and internal pre-amp circuits. The instruments have solid bodies, with neck and body laminated together. There is a large brass block underneath the bridge which increases sustain through its weight. The guitar has three pick-ups: The lead and rhythm are active, while the middle is recessed from the strings and acts as a hum-cancelling coil. It does not have simple pot controls, but uses rather a network of electronic filters for bass and treble. The guitars have switches for playing in phase, out-of-phase, stereo, mono, and for playing with different combinations of pick-ups.

Photographed at the Alembic Shop, San Francisco.

34

B. C. RICH
—'Seagull' 1975
FIG. 43

THIS GUITAR uses two Guild humbucking pick-ups on its mahogany solid-body. There is a six-position varitone control, a built in power booster that has its own volume control and provisions for phasing pick-ups. The pick-ups themselves are linked to a splitter switch which allows use of one-half of a pick-up. The bridge is made by Leo-Quan. This new guitar company is attracting considerable attention with their well crafted and thought out acoustic and electric guitars.

FRAMUS
—'Nashville Standard' 1975
FIG. 44

FRAMUS IS AN old instrument company. Bill Lawrence (acknowledged as perhaps *the* electric guitar genius), for many years worked with Framus to develop their guitars. Bill took a break to work a while for Gibson and then returned to Framus to design a new line of guitars. This guitar shown is one of the simplest of that line. The solid body of this guitar is made of Bavarian larch, a relative of pine. Though the standard has been hardwood, this guitar further opens the door to different materials. The neck is made of maple for strength. There is a six-position selector switch that allows unusual pick-up combinations. These combinations are possible because the dual-coil pick-up can be selected to function as four separate coil pick-ups. It won't be long until many people copy these guitars.

Design Features of Electric Guitars

A GUITAR produces sounds from vibrating strings that are stopped (shortened) at predetermined points along its length. These positions are calculated to produce notes of the European/Western musical scale—A, B, C, D, E, F, G, with half steps (semi-tones) between all notes except B and C, E and F. Semi-tones are A# (A-sharp), B♭ (B-flat) and so forth. Only in theory do, for instance, G♭—one fret space on the guitar before G— and F#—one fret space past F—sound precisely the same. The juggling around of note frequencies to blend harmoniously is called temperament. Owing to its design, the guitar cannot be perfectly tuned, but it can be extremely close. Many people continue to experiment in order to achieve a harmonious scale.

Wire string guitars suffer from poor intonation more than nylon. Intonation is a string sounding the exact frequency required for a particular note. When the strings go from a plain high string of .010 in. diameter to a wound low string of .056 in., each of the strings require a different stopping length in order to sound an octave over the 12th fret. For this reason, all good steel string guitars have a slanted saddle in a bridge that provides different lengths. These lengths, however, are dependent on the gauge and tension of the strings; different size strings require different lengths. Tuning would be made easier with a bridge that could be adjusted to different forward and backward movements, as well as to different heights. But, unfortunately, weight of such a device on the light top of an acoustic guitar would hinder sound production. Since most acoustic musicians do not play much beyond the 12th fret, intonation problems are not very obvious. However, with its multitude of changing diameter strings, an acoustic 12-string is painful to listen to when played past the 12th fret.

Since the electric guitar does not rely on a soundboard to amplify sound, an adjustable bridge is permissable. In fact, with a solid body, the more mass it has, the more it holds played tones, this is called "sustain." And because electrics are commonly played beyond the 12th fret, intonation problems make an adjustable bridge nearly mandatory.

Figs. 45 and 46 Electric guitar bridges.

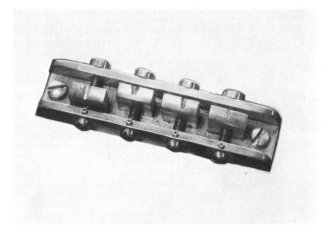

The two most common types of electric guitars are the solid body and the hollow body. The solid body electric is made from solid material, and does not have an acoustic soundbox. Various materials are used—aluminum, wood, stone, plastic—each having its own particular effect on the resultant sound. The design of a guitar's body has a great influence on the sound produced; this design element functions differently in various types of guitars. One person in New Jersey, a Mr. Cawson, recently patented a guitar with a body of solid marble. I'm told the sustain is great, but the weight leaves something to be desired.

Fig. 47 A solidbody guitar, the Harmony H619

Woods used range from light softwoods to very heavy hardwoods. The Telecaster and Les Paul are examples of this solid body type. Some Les Paul guitars have bodies which consist of a solid maple top $\frac{1}{2}$ in. thick carved on the outside, and pieces of mahogany which are laminated onto it. Solid bodies do have cavities to hold components; these cavities are quite large in guitars that have built-in circuit boards, but solid body guitars do not rely on sound chambers to shape the sound.

On a solid body electric, the extra weight helps to balance the guitar when playing, as well as to add sustain.

The hollow body guitar is closer to the acoustic guitar than the solid body. The arched top "F" hole guitars of the jazz and dance band era (20's and 30's) were made electric by attaching pickups. Although the sound of hollow body electrics is electrically amplified, these guitars rely on a sound chamber to "shape" sound. Some hollow bodies are only 1¾ in. thick, some nearly 5 in. Less expensive models use laminated wood for the body, whereas expensive ones have tops and backs carved from solid blocks of wood. Some guitar designers try to place as much of the hardware as possible floating over the top so that it doesn't

interfere with the top's freedom to vibrate. Most hollow body guitars have "F" holes or similar twin soundholes on top. The Gibson ES-345 is an example of this type of guitar.

Fig. 48   Gibson ES-345.

The influence of the soundhole in regard to tone is interesting. Lester Davidson of Martin feels that it is not so much the arched top and back as the shape of "F" holes that give arched "F" guitars their distinctive sound. He showed me an arched top round soundhole Martin, in the process of being restored. He credits "F" holes with sound dispersion qualities, while feeling arched-top roundhole guitars have more of a flat top quality to the sound. "F" holes can have different shapes (are they still "F" holes?): Gibson has a Trini Lopez guitar with diamond-shaped holes. Hollow construction does produce a slight amount of sound. Surprisingly though, when the guitar is amped, the body does not boost sound. Due to the guitar's light weight, the sound produced is quickly dissipated. The energy of the sound leaves the guitar through its soundholes. On the other hand, a heavy solid body guitar recycles the sound adding sustain.

A third type of electric guitar is the acoustic electric, which is simply a normal acoustic with some type of amplification. The Ovation acoustic/electric offers a fine example.

Hardware is an element of the guitar that is usually purchased rather than made by the guitar builder. Tuning machines and bridges are two such pieces of hardware. In addition, many guitars have "tremolo tailpieces" which actually produce vibrato. Arched-top guitars have tailpieces that anchor the strings. Gretsch has advertised a tailpiece on some guitars stating that, "the Chromatic tailpiece reduces tension and equalizes the finger pressure, resulting in an easy flowing playing action." This device allows shorter over-all length strings.

The "heart" of an electric guitar is the fretboard. It is on the fretboard that a skilled guitarist's fingers originate the rising and falling tones which his other hand sets vibrating. The entire length of the fretboard must be level. This allows the strings to be very low (close to the fretboard) enabling fast easy playing, and at the same time preventing a string from buzzing or stopping at the fret in front of the one being fingered. Leveling the fretboard is an exacting job, but can be accomplished with the proper tools.

Unlike the classic guitar with its large wooden neck and gently (comparatively) pulling nylon strings, wire-strung guitars are under more stress. To make matters worse, steel string guitars, to facilitate a different style of playing, have thin necks. The neck must be reinforced to prevent its bending under the load. If you've ever tried to play an inexpensive guitar with a bowed neck that caused the strings to be high above the fretboard, you know how hard fingering can become. Many people do not play steel string guitars because it hurts their fingers: If these people would try a quality electric guitar with extra light gauge steel strings, I'm sure they'd find it as playable as a classical guitar.

Since Martin is the oldest guitar company in the United States, they have had ample time to try various truss rods. Early Martins had a strip of ebony inlaid down the middle of the neck under the fretboard. To add even greater resistance against bending, Martin adopted a "T" section metal rod which ran down the neck, again under the fretboard. More recently, Martin began to use a 3/8 in. hollow square box section instead of the "T". This bar is made to remain rigid, rather than to be adjustable —I have never known a box rod to bend. Necks do, however, slip in the dovetail joint attached to the body, which can give the appearance of the neck bending. Of course, the box rod's effect on guitar weight, sustain, and volume should be considered. This type of rod, in addition, is the easiest to fit into a neck. But since the Martin Company often does not care to sell their rods for anything but bona fide Martin repairs, I will show how to use ordinary mild steel to achieve the same ends.

The patents on Gibson's adjustable truss rod have long-since expired. Guild, Ovation, Fender, and

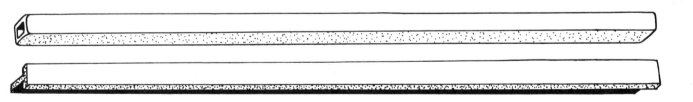

Fig. 49 Drawing of Martin truss rods.

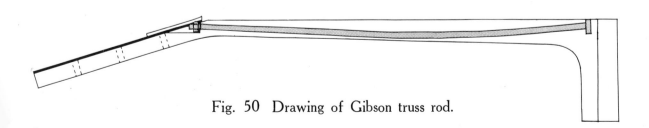

Fig. 50 Drawing of Gibson truss rod.

Gretsch use similar truss rods. There is a channel of varying depth cut in the neck into which a metal rod is placed. At one end, the rod is fastened to keep it from turning, and at the other end there is a nut and washer. A piece of wood is inserted in the neck's groove over the rod; the rod is then passing through a long hole in a wooden neck. When the nut is tightened, force is applied—via the rod's leverage—pulling the neck against the pull of the strings.

The Yamaha Company uses a rod similar to Gibson's but easier to fashion. It goes at a straight taper through the neck. I make my own to any length by welding a square bolt to one end of a fine threaded 3/16 in. rod (available at a hardware store), then cutting the rod to the desired length. I then shape a washer to clear the top of the peghead and use a Gibson truss rod nut. A sleeve of thin plastic tubing (or some other anti-vibration material) should be placed over the rod to prevent its buzzing against the wood.

The Fender Company makes a fine neck out of one piece of maple. There is no separate fretboard —the frets are in the top of the neck. Since it's made from one piece of wood, the neck is consequently more solid than usual. On most guitars, the glue-joint, located on the fretboard and neck,

slips, which allows the neck to bend. In order to insert an adjustable truss rod, Fender routs out a slot from the back of the neck, puts the rod in, and then places a strip of walnut over it.

The Gretsch Company has a wonderful invention — the gearbox on its adjustable rod. The weakest point on a guitar is the area where the fretboard ends and the peg head begins. The wood in this area is very narrow — many a head has broken off when a guitar is dropped. If wood is cut away to make room for an adjustable nut and a wrench, this area has little wood to hold it together. The Gretsch Company, to compensate for this, has placed the means of adjustment on the body-end of their rods. A 16 to 1 gearbox is reached through a hole in the base of the neck. This leaves the thinnest part of the neck as strong as possible.

An adjustable truss rod, invented by the Rickenbacker Company, is thought by many repairmen to be the most successful design. Basically, it consists of a rod that folds back on itself. When the nut is tightened on one rod, it butts against its tail and bends. Rickenbacker puts two of these rods in their guitars so that the neck can be adjusted to pull bass strings more than treble. This type of rod requires an even-depth channel under the fretboard. John Hall of Rickenbacker has told me that they've

Fig. 51 Yamaha neck cut in half.

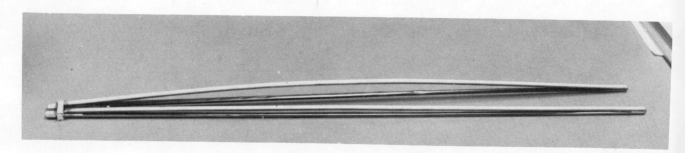

Fig. 52 Rickenbacker truss rods.

never had a guitar neck that couldn't be straightened if the rod was still intact. Some people, though, do break rods by incorrect tightening. In this case, the rod can be slipped out and a new one installed.

The Alembic Company picks right up on the broken rod problem. They make a rod based on one rod tightening against another, similar to Rickenbacker's. They take a great deal of time and expense in making their rods out of very hard stainless steel.

Any of the rod systems mentioned can be used, if installed and adjusted correctly.

The frets must be precisely located and firmly attached. Rickenbacker makes some fretboards with frets that are sloped down on the bass side to facilitate easier playing. It is a fairly standard practice to arch the top of the fretboard to facilitate fretting. Different musicians prefer varying amounts of curve—some a lot, some none at all. The edge of the frets must be smoothed so that a hand can glide easily up and down the neck without catching on any fret ends.

The neck is the foundation of the fretboard and holds the tuning machines by which the strings are stretched to required tension. Necks are often maple or genuine mahogany. It must be slim enough for a hand to get around, but must not bend under string tension.

The purpose of the sloping back angle of a guitar's head is to enable the strings to press firmly against the nut. The head on a Fender guitar does not angle back—rather it dips down evenly; this is a fine alternative. I prefer to make guitars with the end of the head in line with the back. In this way, if the guitar is ever dropped, chances of damage are reduced. The neck can be made more stable if two pieces of mirror-matched wood, split vertically to the neck's end, are used. This helps reinforce the wood against bending in the direction of a weak grain. Tuning machines are used to tighten strings to the proper tension; these are units geared to allow small amounts of turning. Machines should turn without play. Worn or cheap gears make tuning almost impossible.

The body of a guitar, as previously mentioned, contributes to its sound quality and color. The strings attach to it, the electronics fit on or within it. Different materials, such as hard or soft wood, plastic or metal, affect the overall mass, and hence, the sustain. Some materials vibrate more readily at certain frequencies, and so will assist those frequencies more than others.

The "brains" of a guitar are the electric elements. The pulse beat sound is received by these elements and shaped into what you want to play. You can buy some pick-ups and do a standard wiring job, or you can go as far as designing your own pick-ups, pre-amps, and filter circuits.

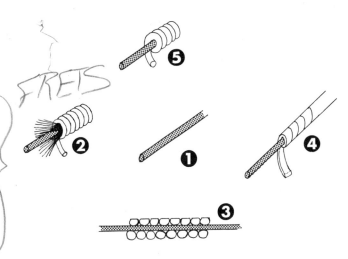

1—Nylon or plain steel
2—Silk&steel
3—Groundwound
4—Flatwound
5—Wire with wire winding, nylon on nylon, or wire on nylon

Fig. 53   Types of string construction.

THERE ARE TWO main types of guitar strings—metal and nylon. Nylon strings have replaced animal gut strings for use on classical and flamenco guitars. There are, however, nylon strings which are actually a filament of nylon wrapped with metal wire; these are used on classical or flamenco guitars for the three lower-pitched strings. Metal strings are used on country-folk guitars such as the Martin D-28. Strings for this type of guitar are made of nickle-silver or of bronze alloys. Bronze gives a coarser, fuller sound which benefits bass notes. The two highest-pitched strings are plain steel, to accent the treble. They are round-wound—that is, the bass strings are made with round wire wrapped around a core wire. For added strength, the core wire is steel alloy like the treble strings. Groundwound strings are available also; these strings have the round wire wrapping ground, thus flattening the coil humps in the strings. This enables the fingers to slide easily over the strings. For acoustic guitars, silk and steel strings are used. These have a wire core with a padding of silk under the outer wire wrapping. The padding brings the exterior dimension up to the size necessary to produce a bass sound. This construction allows for strings which take less pressure to finger.

*   *   *

Finally we come to strings for electric guitars. On guitars that have a piezo-electric transducer or contact mike, any type of string can be used. Guitars with magnetic pick-ups require strings that will affect the magnetic field most efficiently. In this case, nylon won't do at all, and bronze is not as strong and clear as steel alloy strings. Round-wound, ground-wound, and flat-wound strings are available for electrics. The flat-wound type has a winding of flat metal instead of simply round wire. In addition, tape-wound strings are made specifically for electric guitars. These are then wrapped once again with smooth plastic tape, providing a slick, fast surface.

Strings come in various gauge diameters. For convenience, string companies choose sizes to sell together as sets. Sets may be extra-light gauge, light medium, medium heavy, or heavy. Heavier strings last longer, but they are harder (stiffer) and thus, more difficult to finger. The lifetime of a metal string is limited by the rearrangement of molecular structure which eventually reduces its elasticity. This reduction is caused by the string's end-to-end tension which in turn produces a compression across its diameter. It is this compression that re-forms its structure. Aside from this, the single greatest cause of dead strings is the sweat and dirt coming from the player's hands. This premature deadening can be rectified by cleaning strings often. I take my strings off when the bass sounds like slapping a dead trout. Submerging them in a jar of ethyl acetate, I shake them every so often, and let them sit for about one day. I dry them in the air before re-stringing. Acetone, alcohol, or any non-oily solvent will work.

*   *   *

Many guitars incorporate mechanical tailpieces that allow a guitarist to bend notes at will. Tones can be produced that are beyond the restriction of the fretboard scale. Since weight is not necessarily detrimental to an electric guitar, the installation of a fairly heavy vibrato unit is permissible. Paul Bigsby, the co-designer of the Bigsby-Travis guitar, designed and patented the most successful vibrato unit. Many guitar companies make vibrato tailpieces that are incorrectly labeled as tremolo units. The Bigsby unit is made of cast aluminum with a shaft that rotates on needle bearings. This device enables a guitarist to press on a lever and lower the pitch of the strings. Releasing pressure on the lever allows built-in springs to return the strings to previous pitch. Many companies make their own devices under license from Bigsby.

The changing tension of a vibrato unit has a tendency to cause strings to go out of tune. Bigsby's invention, the palm pedal, is mechanically more successful. It provides pedal steel effects on two of the strings.

Fig. 54 A Bigsby vibrato tailpiece.

TWELVE-STRING guitars are more common as acoustic than as electric instruments. Most 12-string electrics have wider fretboards and longer pegheads than 6-string guitars. Whereas most 6-strings have the narrow end of the fretboard between 1½-1⅞ inches wide, 12-string fretboards are often 1¾-2 inches. Closer strings can provide quick chording, while wider spacing allows easier single course fingering. Extending the peghead to take extra individual machines can make it awkward and heavy. Tuning machines for 12-string guitars can be obtained which have two compact banks of machines grouped six in a line. Rickenbacker 12-strings use a combination of six horizontal and six vertical machines to preserve the same size peghead as a 6-string. Since most electric 12-strings are used with super light strings, the stress on the neck is not more than that of a six-string. No massive neck reinforcement is needed. Of course a bridge that accepts 12 strings is necessary.

A six-string pick-up will work satisfactorily with the six courses of a 12-string.

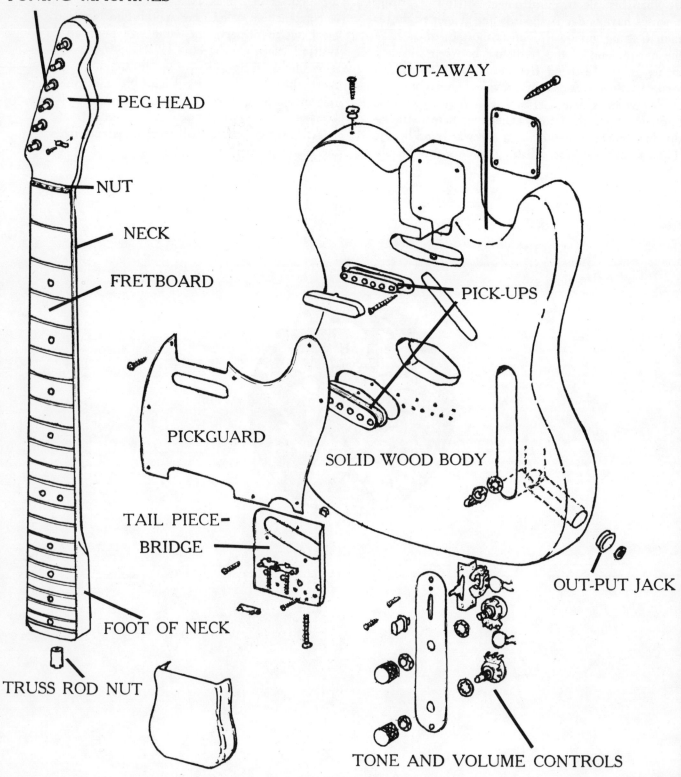

TUNING MACHINES

PEG HEAD

NUT

NECK

FRETBOARD

CUT-AWAY

PICK-UPS

PICKGUARD

SOLID WOOD BODY

TAIL PIECE-
BRIDGE

OUT-PUT JACK

FOOT OF NECK

TRUSS ROD NUT

TONE AND VOLUME CONTROLS

PARTS OF A SOLID BODY GUITAR

Exploded view of a Fender Telecaster

PARTS OF A HOLLOW BODY GUITAR

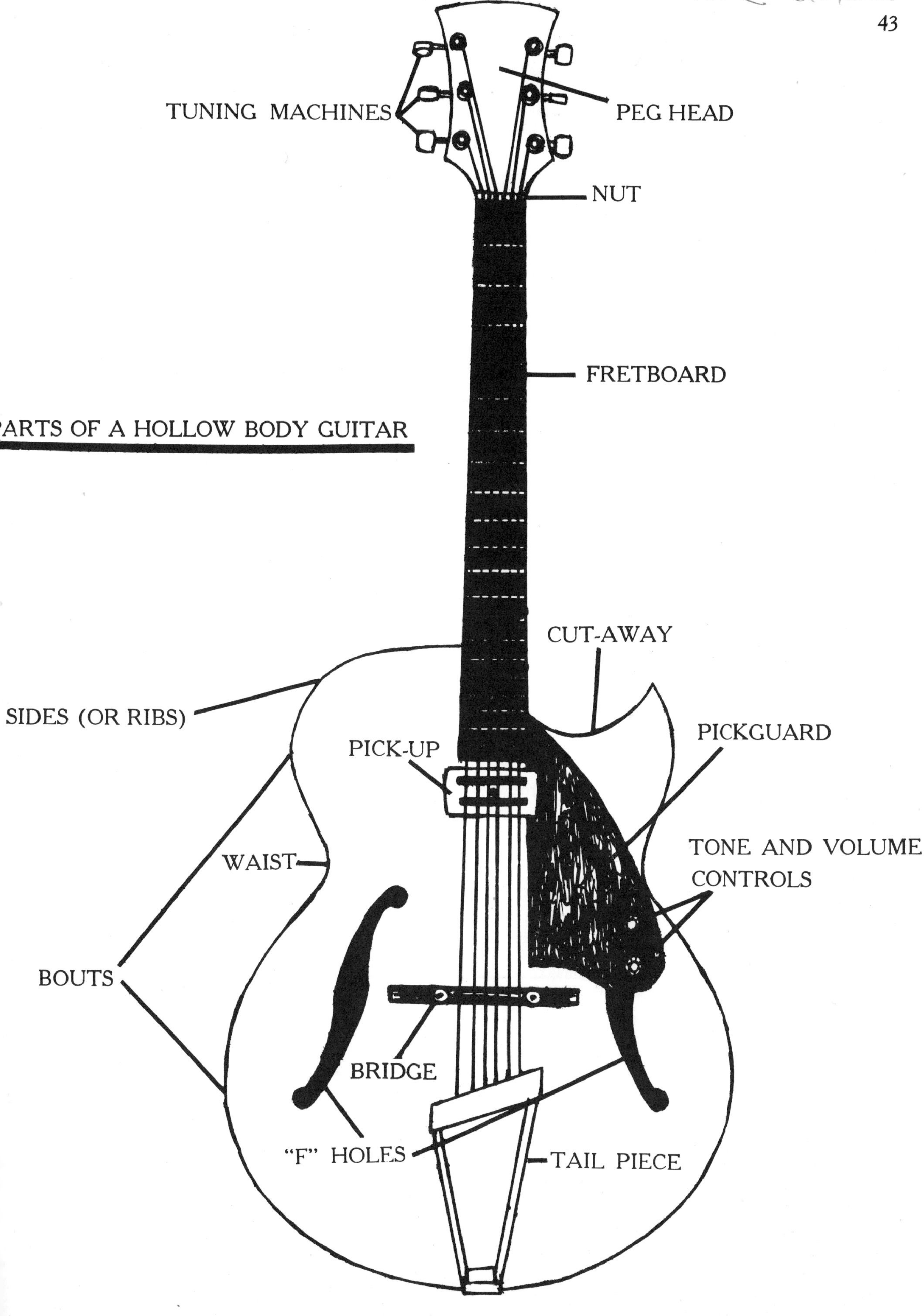

TUNING MACHINES

PEG HEAD

NUT

FRETBOARD

CUT-AWAY

SIDES (OR RIBS)

PICKGUARD

PICK-UP

TONE AND VOLUME CONTROLS

WAIST

BOUTS

BRIDGE

"F" HOLES

TAIL PIECE

Amps & Sound Devices

THE PURPOSE of this section is to give you a basic idea of what an amp is, what it's function is, and what kinds there are. You might say it all began with Geissler, the inventor of the vacuum tube, although many of the basic amp circuits have been patented by Western Electric. With these early circuits frequency response was not perfect, not to mention the imperfection evident in speakers. Technology was of course in its infancy. These days, with men walking on the moon and integrated circuits, amp design can be very complicated indeed!

Fender's first real successes were in the field of amps. Using the rear of his small radio repair shop, he constructed the prototype Fender amp. In 1948, he was joined by Donald Randall and by 1949 they came out with the "Super Amp." Four years later, the Fender Company introduced the "Twin Amp"—a tube unit with two speakers in a cabinet, covered with linen tweed. Many people liked its sound and its (now funky) appearance. It had 45 RMS Watts and was the most powerful made. Since then it has evolved into the present 100 Watt Twin, having lost its too easily torn tweed.

When C.B.S. first took over Fender they started to make solid state amps that were always breaking down and which gave muddy highs. This gave "solid state" a bad name, but C.B.S. has since become very concerned about these problems, and are working now to produce some very fine equipment.

Old Marshalls, Orange, and Sound City amps are among the favorites of many musicians—*Old* because most new products simply are not as good. Ralph Nader *has* made an impact on corporate America: Many companies have become increasingly concerned with quality. If you want good products, complain when you're abused. Some amps which are currently popular include Fender, Traynor, Acoustic, Marshall, Ampeg, Sunn, Cerwin-Vega, GMT, Altec and BGW. Modern solid state circuits are making varieties of sounds now, even "tubey" circuits are added sometimes. The amp and speakers you choose are dependent naturally on the music you're going to play. More power and bigger speakers are necessary for bigger, louder concerts. Large, high-powered systems for use in a small space are in a sense inadequate: Some sound frequencies won't have room to form air waves, and thus certain sounds will be inaudible. Warehouse Sound Company (Railroad Square, San Luis Obisbo, Calif. 93405) puts out a good booklet that discusses what kind of equipment is best for different gigs.

The diagram shows a basic schematic of an amplifier tube. A current is attempting to pass through the vacuum in the tube from the power source input across to the output. There is a grid between these elements. The grid is connected to the pick-up output, which varies in current as a result of string vibration. This varying grid current acts as an opening and closing door to the power supply current. Since the output of a magnetic pick-up is extremely small, a basic amplifier has multiple units such as the pre-amp, voltage amplifier, the phase inverter, and the power output. Though musical instrument amplifiers sacrifice some audio fidelity for power, flat frequency response should be strived for.

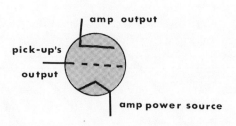

Fig. 55   Diagram of amplifier tube.

SOLID STATE (transistor) elements offer advantages of longer life, economy, and compactness. Early solid state amps were not dependable and did not have the same clear highs that tube units had. With more recent developments, some solid state amps have circuits which imitate tube sound. Other solid state advances have produced I-C's— integrated circuits. These circuits are so miniaturized that an amp circuit is the size of the end of a match. The diagram of a transistor shows its three parts, which behave similarly to the elements in a tube. One great disadvantage of solid state is that it isn't readily serviceable by the user.

coils so that wire can be wound tighter for more sensitive response.

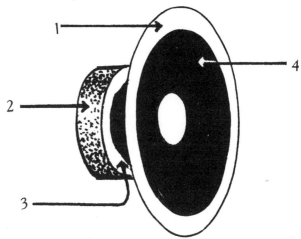

1—Surround (fabric edgings of cone)
2—Magnet and voicecoil structure
3—Spider (fabric support of cone end)
4—Speaker cone

Fig. 57   Diagram of a speaker

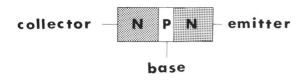

Fig. 56   Diagram of amplifier transistor.

SOME SPEAKERS are ideal for small places, some for large. Some carry only certain frequencies. There are speakers for the bass range (woofers), mid-range, and treble (tweeters). An 18 inch speaker can sound a lower pitch fundamental than a 15 inch, but it must have enough space for the long sound waves to spread. High frequency waves (high pitch) tend to travel in a straight line, whereas waves of low frequency are omni-directional. Notice that high frequency speakers are often made to fan out the sound.

The basic difference between home hi-fi speakers and speakers for instruments is the strength of the spider and surround. The stiffer the spider, the more apparent the trebles. Stiffness also reduces fidelity and low frequency vibrations.

Speaker cones are made of paper, plastic or aluminum. A thin cone will handle trebles more easily, a thick cone, bass sounds. Weight is a factor relating to the work required of a speaker. So, for instance, the voice coils on high frequency units are often wound with aluminum wire instead of heavier copper. Altec uses flattened wire for voice

Compression driver horns, usually part of a P.A. system, are not strong enough for guitars. But horns are being developed, however, for high loads. The horns themselves are often made from metal or plastic. Metal horns, though, such as cast aluminum, present problems, especially if they are not properly dampened. In this case, they will ring like a bell at their natural resonating frequency. Wooden horns, similar to the ones at Capricorn Sound Studio in Georgia, are used for custom sound systems.

Whatever the sound system used, it is imperative that the impedances be matched. If you were to use an eight ohm speaker system with a two ohm amp, you would certainly have problems. Since P equals E squared divided by I (where P is watts, E is volts, and I is resistance), it is evident that a solid state, low impedance amp with low impedance speakers will provide you with more watts to make sound. Lower impedance is translated to low resistance.

Speaker grills are also important since they protect the cones and, in addition, have a bearing on sound. Cloth grills have a tendency to absorb trebles; they also rattle, creating a snare drum effect. The new foam grills, which don't rattle, are far more transparent to sound.

FOR THE GREATEST possible range of sound and expression when using a guitar, a number of sound embellishment devices may be used. Although the best devices, if used by inexperienced guitarists, cannot make them sound competent, skilled players can benefit greatly from the expansion of style they offer.

Alembic makes guitars and amps that are very versatile but, unfortunately, very expensive. However, with some time and patience, it is possible to build a comparable guitar with low impedance pick-ups, pre-amp coupled with boosters, and filter devices. I encourage you to learn how to make your own circuits. There are I-C hobby kits available which relate to guitar electronics.

* * *

The S. Hawk Company and I.S.C. Audio, both of New York, are two companies which have made sound devices worthy of note. The former company makes three sound embellishment devices:

1. A linear pre-amp with fuzz and sustain.

2. A bass range expander that functions as a graphic equalizer, an upper bass harmonic booster, and pre-amp. There are also separate controls for the high and low strings.

3. A tonal expander with three boost or cut positions — bass, mid-range, and treble contour — which offers an infinite variety of tonal responses.

I.S.C. Audio makes a guitar-synthesizer combination. (Nothing would please me more than if someone reading this book were to make something like this). The guitar is an all mahogany solid body with one pick-up that feeds a synthesizer/amp. It works very much like an electric organ: There are control levers which allow for selection of sounds imitating other instruments, such as violin, flute and harpsichord. This type of unit shapes an incoming signal with filter, choke, and booster circuits. Different instruments have various portions of harmonics and fundamentals emphasized. Controls which filter out or boost selected frequencies, as well as lengthen or shorten sustain, can be used to copy tonal profiles of other instruments.

* * *

Wah-Wah—This device emphasizes a specific band of frequencies. Movement of a pedal control moves that band of frequencies up or down the audio spectrum. An R.L.C. network is used to select the frequency band which, in turn, is fed into a feed-back amplifier. The band is moved by varying the feed-back. The Wah-wah is used between the guitar and the amp.

Phaser—This is also used between the guitar and amp. Variations in output frequency are produced by an instantaneous changing in phase of the original signal. This produces a Doppler train whistle effect: That is, when a train blowing its whistle comes towards you, passes, then goes in the opposite direction, the frequency of the whistle seems to change. The signal varies the resistance of an R.C. network, thus providing phase shift dependent on frequency; the output of this network combined with the input signal results in phase shift. The electronic circuit consists of integrated circuits.

Vibrato—This is simply the rhythmic variations of frequency. The warble in a singer's voice is vibrato. Vibrato devices, usually changing frequency by about 5-10%, have one control for speed of frequency, and another for intensity.

Tremolo—This is the rhythmic variation of sound level. Tremolo devices momentarily soften the volume, then make it louder.

Boosters—These work mainly by filtering out selected frequencies, and boosting the harmonic tones of others. There are usually controls for intensity.

Reverb—This device is often mechanical rather than electronic. A long metal spring vibrates with frequencies fed into it (and continues to vibrate) giving off the original signal with an echo which is fed to an output.

Electric Guitar Pick-ups

THE REASON for making your own pick-ups is similar to why you might want to build your own guitar. There are many fine pick-ups made however, and it is not a simple matter to make a pick-up. It is helpful to have some working knowledge of D.C. resistance, impedances of different frequencies in induction coils, and gauss/flux fields. I do not mean to scare you off, but pick-up making is not just wrapping any amount of any copper wire around any magnet structure.

Early pick-ups used large cobalt magnets. The Gibson magnet is an example of a cobalt magnet pick-up. There is an iron plate that comes up from

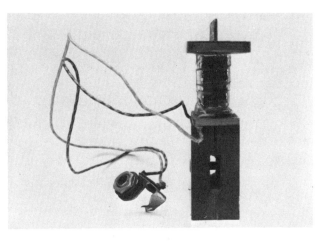

Figs. 58 and 59 Believed to be the pick-up used on the first Gibson electric guitars.

the magnet. The top edge of the plate would be positioned under an instrument's steel strings. A coil of copper wire is wound around the plate and has a piece of poplar above it which is pierced by the plate. This creation weighs 1 lb. 8 oz. Magnets in those days were not very powerful, large ones were needed to drive the low powered amps then available.

Early Rickenbacker guitars had pick-ups that were made with two horseshoe-shaped tungsten steel magnets. The tungsten steel was made magnetic by being positioned in an intense electrical current for a lengthy amount of time. Between the magnets there is a coil of copper wire wrapped around six iron pole pieces that are conductive to the flux field. The pole pieces contact the bottoms of the horseshoes. The strings pass through a very strong field between the tops of the magnets. The large tungsten magnets were only discontinued when tungsten became unavailable.

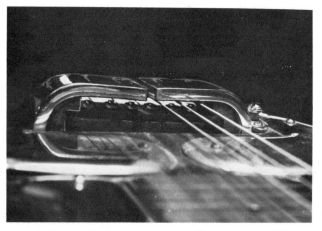

Fig. 60 Close-up of pick-up on an old Rickenbacker guitar.

The pole magnet pick-ups on Fender guitars are a wonder of simplicity and success. The six alnico magnets are held by fiberboard. The size of the magnets in a Stratocaster pick-up are approximately 3/16 x 5/8 in. Alnico stands for Aluminum, Nickel and Cobalt. Alnico is a powerful permanent magnet alloy containing iron, nickel, aluminum and

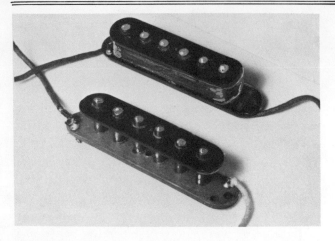

Fig. 61   Fender pick-ups.

one or more of the elements cobalt, copper and titanium. A copper coil is wound around the bare magnets. Some Fender pick-ups use staggered height magnets so that some strings have more emphasis. The depth and the size of the coils have an effect on sound. The Jazzmaster has short, fat coils, while the Jag has long, thin coils. A fat coil will have the outside windings affected less than the inner windings. A Strat pick-up has 7,600 turns of 42 gauge plain enamel wire. A Tele lead uses 7,800 turns of No. 42 while the Rhythm gets No. 43. The D.C. resistance of a Tele is 6,000 Ohms. After the wire is wound, the units are dipped in wax to seal them and then, on most Fender guitars, put in a plastic case. A copper clad plate is put on the bottom and leads of No. 22 stranded copper wire with BTPVC wrapping are attached.

THE ROWE Company makes many types of pick-ups, in fact more than 24 different models. Most of Rowe's pick-ups are similar to Fenders, but they do have some refinements and the Rowe is much older than Fender. The pick-up shown is Model RHC-B. I have used and abused it for years. It seems indestructible. I have had to resolder wires I have torn over the years, however. The magnet for the second string is recessed from the top to give a more even string response. On model 210 the magnets have aluminum threads bonded to them. These magnets can be adjusted in height to the strings by screwing in or out of a plastic bobbin that the copper coil is wound around. This is the bottom of the Rowe pick-up for the D-28E. Note the screw-adjusted grippers holding the magnets.

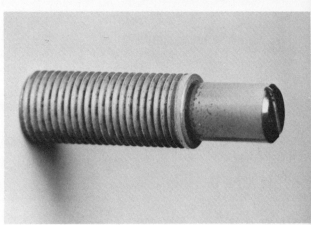

Fig. 63   Rowe magnet with bonded threads.

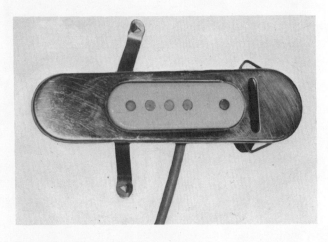

Fig. 62   Rowe RHC-B pick-up.

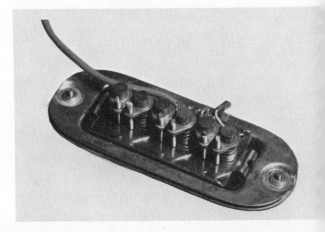

Fig. 64   Bottom of Rowe pick-up for the D-28E

The Rowe Company also makes pick-ups for ukes, violins, autoharps, pianos, and more. They now make a humbucking pick-up that can be attached to an acoustic guitar.

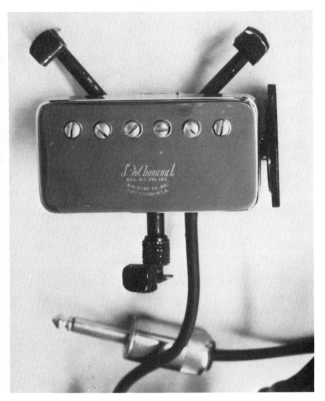

Fig. 65 A Rowe clip-on humbucking pick-up.

Fig. 66 Rickenbacker humbucking pick-ups in stages of assembly.

THIS RICKENBACKER pick-up is beautiful in its design and in the painstaking detail of its components. The pick-up starts with a very large, powerful alnico magnet. The magnet is placed on an aluminum base with iron cores flanking it. There are threaded holes in one core for screws to adjust the response of various strings. A plastic bobbin is placed on the cores. The coils are 54 gauge wire. This is by far the finest diameter wire any company I have been to uses. The finer the wire the more windings that can be done close to the magnet's field. The thinner the wire the easier it breaks; because of its trickiness most companies only go to about No. 44. After the coils are assembled they are wrapped in copper tape to shield from R.F. hum. The pick-up is now encapsulated in epoxy to keep moisture out. The pick-ups receive a final plastic case. Attention to the job of the pick-up does not stop here. The cavities inside the guitar where the pick-ups will be, are coated with conductive paint to further shield the pick-ups. The resistance of both coils is 8,500 Ohms.

One problem with humbucking style pick-ups is that the high impedance of the coils results in some high frequency loss. There is a feeling that humbucker's lost highs make them sound muddy when two such guitars share playing lead. Some feel they are better used to play a rich rhythm passage.

Gibson is not resting on its laurels at all. The new epoxy encapsulated high output, ceramic magnet super humbucking pick-up is just one new development of Gibson engineers.

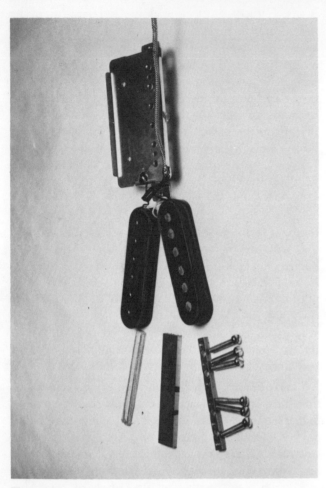

Fig. 67   Gibson pick-up with elements displayed.

CURRENTLY, late 1974 that is, Alembic is making humcanceling low impedance pick-ups that are fed into a pre-amp in the instrument so equipped. Alembic has used both alnico and ceramic magnets. The ceramic matrix material they use is marketed under the trade name Arnox and only comes in bar configurations. Alembic feels that the stronger the magnetic field the better able the pick-up is to receive all the string overtones producing a fuller sound. The current guitar pick-ups on Alembic guitars start as two ceramic magnets on a non-ferrous base. The magnets, each roughly ½ x ½ x 1¼ inches are glued at an angle to the base. The angle enables the pick-up response to be more even than it would be if there were a single bar. The magnets are glued in place on angled shims with an Alpha Cyanoacrylate glue. Fish paper for insulation is wrapped around them and then a copper coil is wound on top of that with anywhere from 30 to 44 gauge wire depending on sound shape desired.

The wire they use is specially coated so that when it is dipped in alcohol the surface sizing melts and then reforms, gluing the wire together. Solidity of the pick-up is necessary to avoid it being microphonic. If the pick-up parts are loose and move they cut lines of magnetic flux and produce a current change in the pick-up, and so, noise. Now a brass, non-conductive, mounting plate is added and a mini co-axial cable lead is wired on. The unit is now wrapped in copper foil for shielding.

Using a silicon rubber mold the unit is encapsulated in polyurethane resin. The mold was formed around a wooden pattern of the desired final pick-up. A and B parts of resin are mixed and put in the mold at room temperature. The unit is quickly inserted in the resin. It is ready to demold in about 15 minutes.

GRETSCH HAS three basic styles of pick-ups—the Supertron (available in Models I and II), the Filtertron and the HI-LO tron. These are humbucking type pick-ups. Ray Butts worked with Chet Atkins to create the Filtertron. This pick-up has a separate coil for each string. Gretsch pioneered stereo for guitar in about 1965 when they took twin leads off a pick-up. This was accomplished by splitting a pick-up so that half of it picked up the lower strings and had its leads while the other half picked up the high three strings and had its leads forming a second channel.

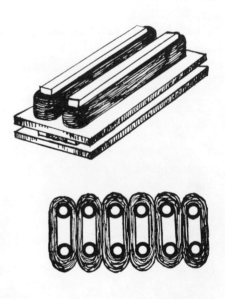

Fig. 68   Drawing of Gretsch pick-ups.

Making Your Own Pick-up

THE FIRST step in making your own pick-up is to set up your criteria. Do you want a high or low impedance unit? Pete Mundy of Aembic divides impedance as such: Low impedance 1,000 to 4,000 coil turns, medium impedance 4,000 to 6,000, and high impedance over 6,000. Pedal Steels are of very high impedance. With lower impedances the signal to noise ratio is worse. John Hall has told me that low impedance pick-ups are not as sensitive to hum, but the leads will have to be shielded. It is important to note that the closer the pick-up is to a pre-amp, the less hum there is. The reason that most pick-ups today are high impedance is that the tube amps could not handle low impedance which requires high amplification. Today's solid state units can. When there are less windings or larger diameter wire to reduce impedance, a loss in output gain will result unless stronger magnets are used. You can use No. 30 wire for a low impedance pick-up or up to No. 54 (if you could wind it without breaking) for a high impedance, high-strength pick-up. Enameled copper magnet wire is the standard material. Since magnet wire breaks easily I suggest that if you are new to this, use no finer gauge than 42. You must remember to match the impedance of your pick-up with that of your amp.

The reason for a pre-amp in a guitar with a low impedance pick-up is to reduce hum. If you are not into electronics, I suggest you make a high impedance pick-up which most common electric guitars and amps have.

What kind of magnets? The stronger the magnets the easier it is to make a strong response pick-up. Alnico has been the standard material for years. It comes in many configurations. There has been a development of it over the years and the commonly used formula is Alnico Type Five. There are various high strength ceramic magnets used. Ceramic is brittle, and made in limited shapes. They come in a wide price range, some cost more, some less, than Alnico. There is a new magnetic material that can be formed in a variety of shapes. A ¼ in. high, ¼ in. wide cylinder goes for about $15. With rhythm, lead, and hum-canceling coil, you could spend $270. on magnets alone. For a low impedance high output, samarium cobalt would be useful. If magnets are too strong they will pull the strings and cause wolf tones.

Shown are the steps in the creation of an Alembic pick-up. Refer to the major companies pick-up photographs in the preceding pages to see alternate styles.

I assume you do not have a winding machine. It is possible to spend several days winding, or you can put the pick-up in the chuck of a variable speed drill and rig a wire feed system. I encourage you to make your own pick-ups and devise your own winding system.

I have known people who have hand-wrapped magnets. My interest in electric guitars began years ago when my brother hand-wound the pick-ups for his first electric guitar.

If you can make your own pick-ups you can do things that are not usually possible, like separate leads for each string. This can allow phasing and tone controls for each individual string.

Shown are some of the possible combinations of pole and bar magnets. The construction of a coil is shown. The way a pick-up works is that the vibrating string is of a ferrous base and is affected by, and affects in turn, the pick-up. The movement of the string results in a changing magnetic field which induces a variable current in the coil which is fed to an amp.

Fig. 69   Alnico and ceramic bar magnets.

Fig. 70   The old Alembic coil winding machine.

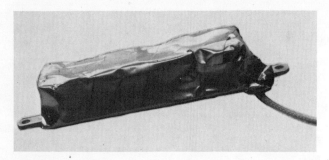

Fig. 71   After the coil is wound and leads are attached, it is wrapped in copper foil.

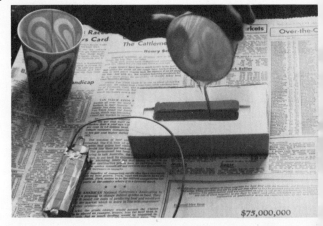

Fig. 73   Resin is poured in a silicon rubber mold

Fig. 74   The pick-up inserted in resin.

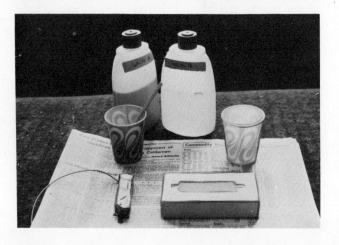

Fig. 72   Materials for encapsulating the pick-up.

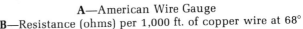

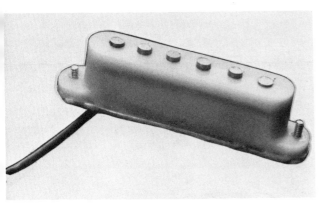

Figs. 75   The pick-up out of the mold.

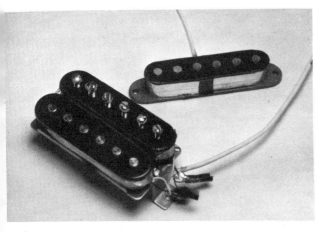

Fig. 76   A Gibson and Fender pick-up with extra shielding added by author.

A—American Wire Gauge					
B—Resistance (ohms) per 1,000 ft. of copper wire at 68°					
A	B	A	B	A	B
25	32.37	32	164.1	39	831.8
26	40.81	33	206.9	40	1049
27	51.47	34	260.9	41	1323
28	64.90	35	329.0	42	1673
29	81.83	36	414.8	43	2104
30	103.20	37	523.1	44	2672
31	130.10	38	659.8	45	3348

Fig. 78   Gauge and wire resistance for plain copper wire.

Unfortunately, piezo-electric pick-ups are rather complex, and I do not feel I could cover the construction so that an amateur could build a respectable unit.

* * *

As STATED earlier, Gibson invented the humbucking pick-up. The coils of a humbucking pick-up are wired in parallel so they are, in relationship to each other, out-of-phase. R.F. (Radio Frequency) hum is received by each of these coils. When the signal from each of these coils is joined, the two out-of-phase signals, in effect, cancel each other. This is comparable to a line of ocean waves with

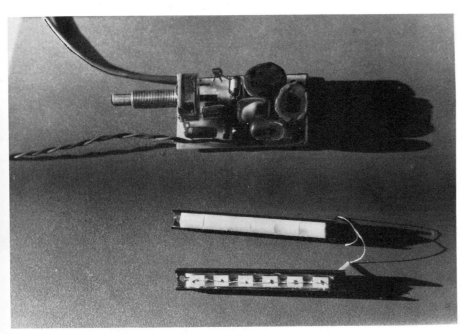

Fig. 77   Ovation piezoelectric pick-up and pre-amp.

an even distribution of crests and troughs intersecting with a second set of waves evenly out-of-step. The crests of the first line pushing against the troughs of the other would smooth each other's impulses. The troughs of the first line pulling against the crests of the second would smooth those impulses.

The string vibration signals received by the magnets would also cancel each other if the polarities were the same while the coils (which receive the induced signals) were wired out-of-phase. If the magnets are of opposite polarities, the humcanceling (parallel) wiring circuit puts them back in phase.

NOTE ON MAGNETIC PICK-UP PHASING

I prefer the ground lead of a pick-up to be the

outside winding of its coil; with separate ground attached to the magnet(s) for optimum quiet operation. One added benefit of an outside ground may be the formation of an electrostatic shield around the coil. However, some pick-up designers believe that the *inside* coil wire should be the ground since it could act as the magnet's ground as well.

It is important to know the magnet polarities of pick-ups to be used together so you can be sure about phasing. A compass held against a pick-up is a good indication device.

The blue wire on a Tele lead pick comes from the *out*side of the coil, the yellow comes from the *in*side. Blue is ground, yellow is hot.

The white wires on a Gibson Humbucking should be wired together and be the hot (live) wire. The black wires should be wired together for the ground.

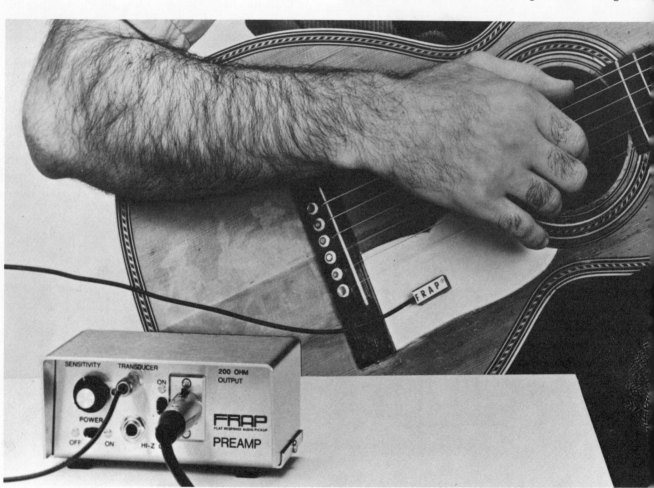

Fig. 79   *Frap*

Construction of Electric Guitars

FOR WHAT REASONS should you build your own guitar? What many musicians want is a combination of various guitars. It is a fact that different people like different features and different sounds in guitars. It is good to keep in mind how subjective music is and how difficult it is to say this is a good guitar and that is a bad guitar.

One of the most valuable aspects of building your own guitar is that you can learn how it works. Another is saving yourself a considerable amount of money by only paying for the expense of the parts. It will take time, but keep in mind that your guitar can be precisely made for you. It's quite a thrill to play a guitar with your name on it.

The selection of wood in regard to its appearance and effect on sound production is difficult to describe in words. Basically wood should be free of warpage, knots and cracks. Wood should be kiln dried. Green wood (freshly cut) shrinks, warps and cracks quite often in the process of drying. If wood is only air dried you are guessing how dry it is. Kiln drying is precision drying to a specific moisture content. All quality solid body guitars are constructed of hardwood. The most common are mahogany, alder, ash and maple. Rosewood, ebony, oak and zebra wood have been used also. What is desired is a dense wood that is dimensionally stable. The density of wood affects the sound produced. The stiffer the wood the brighter the sound, and the heavier the wood the longer it will hold the sound. Hollow body guitars will sometimes have carved softwood tops, but the same characteristics of the wood in solid bodies is applicable.

Guitars are often put together with only glue. Some guitars, such as Fenders, have necks fastened with screws however. Surfaces of wood to be glued must be clean and fit flush. The glue works by penetrating the wood and then hardening. Little hooks, so to speak, of dried glue hold the wood together. Good glues are stronger than the wood itself. When gluing hardwoods it is good to give the glue a chance to seep in. If you apply the glue to hardwood and quickly clamp very tightly, all the glue can be squeezed out, and a weak joint will result. Heat and moisture will break down most glues. This quality can be used to advantage in repairing instruments. A damaged fretboard can be heated with an iron, and a pallet knife inserted to lift it off so that it can then later be replaced.

THE FOLLOWING ARE WOOD APPLICABLE GLUES:

Aliphatic Resin: Similar to ordinary white glue, but stronger. It is water-based, and can be broken down by heat and/or moisture. It has a strong tack and is quick setting.

Casein Glue: Some glue companies combine Casein with vinyl and other ingredients to make a water base glue that is similar to aliphatic glue. Elmers is a Casein-polyvinyl glue.

Epoxy: Some epoxy is good for metal but weak for wood. Check *Consumer's Report*, February, 1974. Epoxy needs to cure at 90-180 deg. to develop full strength. Fast-dry versions are not as strong as the ordinary version. Epoxy will not weaken to permit guitar repairs if a part needs to be taken apart.

Fish Glue: An animal-based glue. This and hide glue were a mainstay of woodworking until the invention of plastic glues. It is water based, and has a slow setting time, allowing for less rushed assembly than white glue. It is broken down by heat, moisture and micro-organisms that may grow in the glue of a joint.

Hide Glue: Similar to fish glue. Proper gluing requires heating glue to an exact constant temperature. Some instrument builders prefer this glue because of its slow setting time and its breakdown characteristics that facilitate repairs. I prefer it for acoustic instruments.

Polyvinyl Acetate: This glue is similar to Casein glue. The word 'poly' means many, and glue companies mix vinyl with other oil-derived ingredients to produce similar glues. Consult tech sheets by specific glue companies in regard to their products.

Powdered Resin: A powdered resin of ureaformaldehyde that is mixed with water to make glue. A very strong glue; many varieties are waterproof. It will not break down for repairs. This glue needs a room temperature of 70 deg. or above to form a strong joint. Fast setting but good to keep clamped for 12 to 24 hours.

Resorcinol Glue: A two part-resin and catalyst-glue which is very strong and completely waterproof. Use above 70 deg. Contains para-formaldehyde which is irritating to eyes, nose, throat and skin. Can not be broken down for instrument repairs.

Tips on Gluing:

1. Soft woods and hardwoods that are carefully machined require 50 PSI clamping pressure. Correct pressure squeezes out air pockets, makes an intimate contact of surfaces to be bonded, and holds parts while the adhesive cures.

2. Recommended Clamping Times at Various Temperatures:

P.R.G.	70 deg.	80 deg.	90 deg.	100 deg.
	13 hrs.	8 hrs.	5 hrs.	3¼ hrs.

Resorcinol
Sets ⅓ quicker

Maximum strength develops in 24-48 hours. White glue sets in 25 to 45 minutes at 70 deg.; maximum strength is achieved within 72 hours.

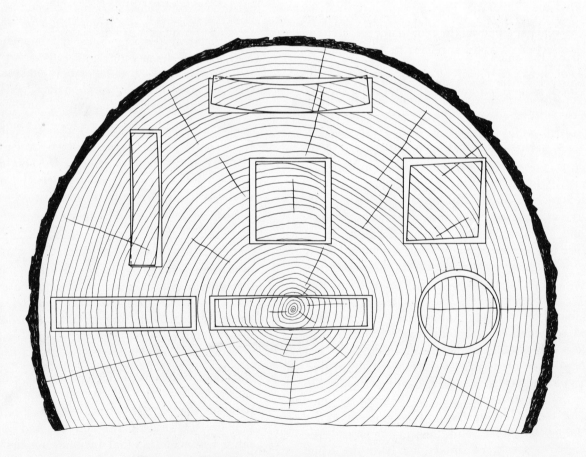

Fig. 80   Shrinkage characteristics of lumber depends on how it is cut. Reproduced courtesy of the U.S. Forest Products Laboratory.

Making A Solid-Body Guitar

THIS SOLID BODY guitar, shown in the process of construction, is made of maple. Apart from tonal considerations, maple's advantage is that it does not need to have its grain filled in order to produce a smooth finish. The neck on this guitar is screwed onto it and is not glued. A bolted-on neck is easy to replace and makes the guitar collapsible for storing. A point to remember is that a guitar should be balanced. A heavy ebony neck with a light mahogany body would be awkward to hold. These considerations of balance have prompted me to make a heavy non-adjustable truss rod on the solid body and a lighter adjustable rod on the hollow body. The added weight aids tonal sustain on the solid body.

Gibson necks join with a similar shaped fit, but are glued in and finished with the body as one unit. The guitars made by Alembic have the neck extend through the body, with the body made of pieces of wood attached to the sides of this extended neck.

To make the neck, laminate two pieces of wood together. Use a jointer or sanding board to produce perfectly flush gluing edges. The reason for laminating is to have the wood's grain oppose itself so it resists warpage in one direction. The wood should be book-matched. Glue this together with P.R.G. or Epoxy. This should never come apart. Slices of alternating varied coloured hardwood can be added to further strengthen and embellish the neck. A center fillet can also be of use in alignment of a reinforcing rod channel and neck to body assembly. You can glue large blocks or cut out the rough shape of the neck before gluing.

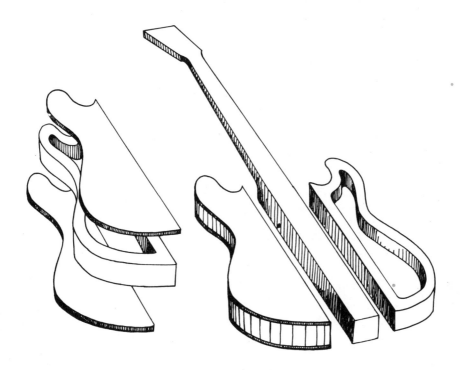

Fig. 81   Alembic assembly method.

Fig. 82 Bandsawing out the side profile of neck.

Fig. 83 Joining the two neck halves.

Fig. 84 Wood cut for a solid body guitar.

Now cut the reinforcement channel. A table saw is easiest to use, but a power router or router plane could be used. Make sure the top of the neck is flush before cutting the channel. The rods shown are two pieces of 5/16 in. square mild steel.

Fig. 85   Dado cutting a channel for neck reinforcement.

Further layout can be done on the neck, which can then be trimmed on a bandsaw. Sand the peghead flat and glue on a veneer. Shape the veneer to the head design. Shape the part of the neck that joins the body. This shaping of the foot can be best done with a bandsaw and files.

Use a drill press to cut perpendicular peg holes according to the placement you draw on the veneer.

Rough form the curve of the neck back with a spoke-shave or drawknife. Use rasps and files for rough finishing. The neck will not be finished until after the fretboard is clamped and glued.

Fig. 86   Rough neck with steel rods and drawing of shape.

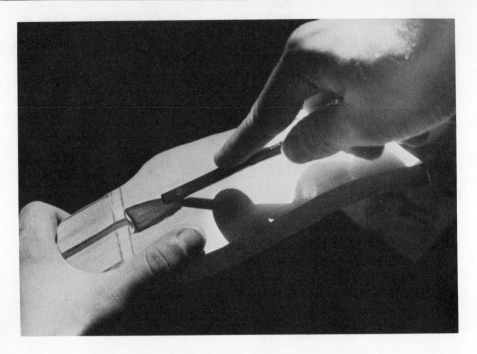

Fig. 87   Carving a notch for an adjustable rod's nut.

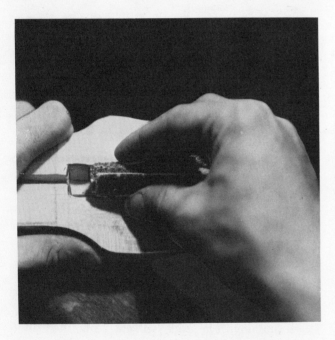

Fig. 88   Finishing the notch with sandpaper.

Fig. 89   Drilling tuning machine holes.

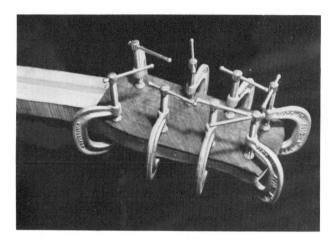

Fig. 91   Clamping a head veneer. You may wish to use a clamping caul on top of veneer

Fig. 90   Cutting out neck shape on bandsaw.

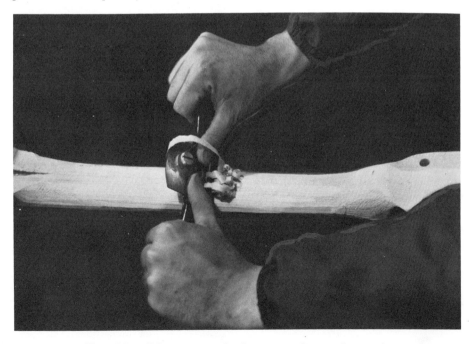

Fig. 92   Using a spokeshave to shape the neck.

Fig. 93   Finishing the back of the peg head.

Fig. 94   Trimming the heel.

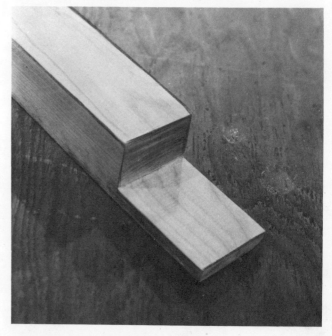

Fig. 95   Centerpiece with notch cut to receive end of neck.

Now it is time to work on the body. Notch the center piece to receive the neck. Glue the two side blocks with PRG to the center as shown. Lay out the body shape, and use a bandsaw to cut it out. As with all woodworking, the more accurate you are in the preliminary stages, the less work you will have later on.

Fig. 96   Gluing the wood for the body together.

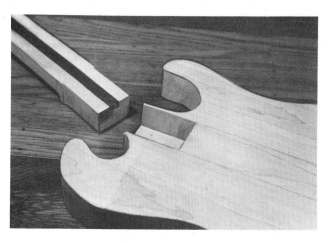

Fig. 98   The neck and body cut to fit.

Fig. 97   The body bandsawed to shape.

Fit the neck to the body without gluing. Drill pilot holes for the four screws that will hold the neck in place. Install the screws. Use rubber cement to temporarily hold the fretboard on. Use strings as guides down each side of the board to center the components. Measure the distance from the nut to the 12th fret. This distance plus 1/32 in. from the 12th fret in the opposite direction is where the treble "E" string should be stopped. Extend the adjustable stop as far forward as it can go; This allows more distant positioning for the other strings. Mark where to drill pilot holes for the bridge mounting screws. Drill holes for the strings. The bridge's front edge (of the plate) should be perpendicular to a line coming down the center of the fretboard. Install metal string stops in the holes in the back of the guitar.

Lay out the installations of pick-up controls and the wiring. Use a router to cut these cavities. Different components require different depths, measure the equipment you use. Use a shaped router cutter to round the edge of the body. The body could be routed from the back with only the pick-ups and control knobs showing, like a Les Paul. The method shown, using a pick guard/cover plate, was chosen for simplicity in construction and accessibility to all components.

Lay out the area of the plate so it covers all the cavities. Make a template of this area. Cut

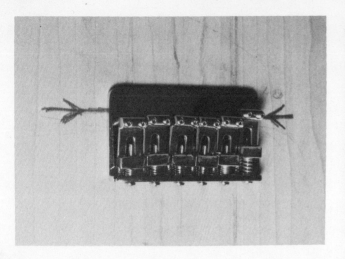

Fig. 99   Positioning the bridge.

Fig. 100   Template and layout for pickguard and internal elements.

Fig. 101   Drilling mounting and string holes for bridge.

material for this; any strong substance will work— plastic and aluminum are the most common. Shown is black plastic. Cut out all necessary openings and trial fit with small mounting screws you have made pilot holes for. Now proceed to chapters on wiring and finishing.

The pickguard must be no more than 1/20 in. thick, or the plastic pick-up holder shown will have to be thinned.

Fig. 102 Rounding the body with a router and concave cutter.

Fig. 103 The body with routed compartments.

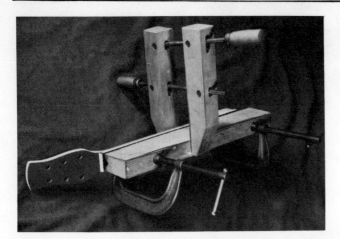

Fig. 104   Gluing the fretboard.

Fig. 105   Installing the neck.

Fig. 106   A jack and the necessary hole.

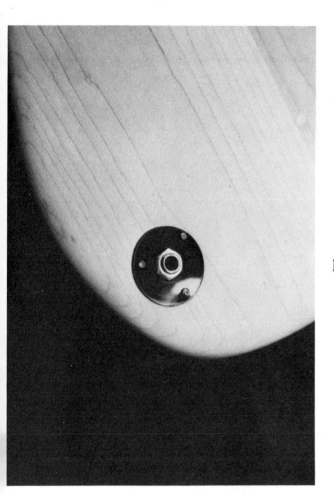

Fig. 107 The jack and plastic mounting plate.

Fig. 108 The completed solid body guitar

Making A Hollow-Body Guitar

THIS CHAPTER explains how to construct a simple hollow body guitar. The construction of this guitar is fairly unconventional. This construction is used to allow the building of a hollow body electric guitar by those persons not blessed with a copious supply of woodworking tools and time. On the most expensive hollow body electrics, the arched top and back are carved from solid blocks of wood. The least expensive would use any type of plywood available. Nearly all plywood hollow bodies have the top and back shaped to an arched configuration by heat, moisture and pressure.

This guitar shown being made uses simple thin hardwood plywood that is held in shape by a combination of elements inside the guitar. To make a carved guitar is to indulge in a very complex, time-consuming project—too involved for the scope of this book. I suggest to those persons so interested to consult information on violins and related instruments. There is monumental knowledge available concerning their carved plates. Metal dies are needed for the efficient forming of arched plates from thin solid wood or plywood. The construction of dies is outside the realm of the individual builder.

Fig. 109 Tapered dovetail slot on a Harmony guitar body.

Fig.110 Tapered dovetail cut on end of a Harmony guitar neck.

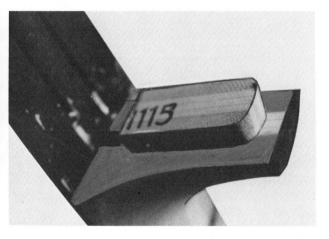

Fig.111 The straight dovetail on an Ovation neck.

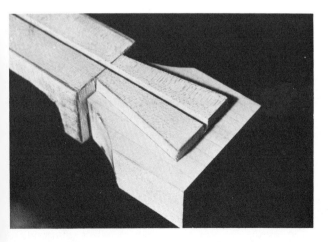

Fig.112 A simple straight dovetail for this book's hollow body guitar.

The fretboard is exactly the same as for the solid body. In joining the neck and body I show an alternate method to the bolted neck, a simple dovetail joint. The arm of the neck, and the basic peghead design is the same, but the foot of the neck terminates in a dovetail. To make the neck, glue two surfaced pieces of book-matched maple together. If the top is not flush after gluing, trim on a jointer. Now cut the channel for the truss rod. It should be 3/16 in. wide and 3/8 in. deep. The truss rod shown is similar to a Rickenbacker rod. One rod tightens against another, which causes the unit to bend opposite the string pull: That is, it does if the short rod that is butted against is on the top! Use 3/16 in. fine thread steel rod that accepts a Gibson rod nut; grind the threads flat along the short top rod so the two rods can slide against each other. Weld the opposite end to the bolt and washer together. You can grind down a larger washer or make one out of sheet metal. The channel is easily cut on a table saw. To make the rod's nut adjustment notch, use chisels and sandpaper. Check for clearance of a rod tightening wrench. Make a nut cover out of plastic or wood and attach with a small screw.

Lay out the neck profile. Cut out with a bandsaw. I used a bandsaw to cut the dovetail block. The fit of the dovetail must be precise on the angled edges. Rough shape the neck with a spokeshave. Complete the head in the fashion used for the solid body.

Cut curved pieces for the body cut-aways. These pieces must fit snugly against the dovetail block. The use of hardwood with the grain appearing as flat layers running parallel to the top and back is recommended.

Any wood can be used for the tailblock that is strong enough to hold the ends of the sides together and accept a tail pin.

To make the sides, cut wood in strips 1/8 in. thick and 1 1/2 in. wide that match the wood of the plates. I use an electrically heated bending pipe for shaping sides. A propane torch is an alternative heat source. I use a 15 in. length of 3 in. diameter cast iron sewer pipe. For pale woods 300 degrees is a good non-scorching temperature; dark wood can take 500 deg. To bend wood, wet it with a water-soaked sponge and press with a rocking motion against the pipe. The heat makes wood pliable and water prevents burning. It helps to have a template to check the sides against.

Fig. 113 Using a hot metal pipe as a bending iron
to shape guitar sides

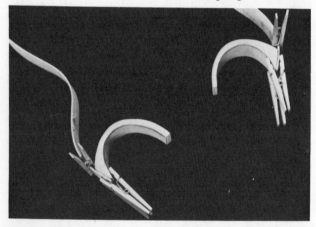

Fig. 114 Gluing cut-away shapes to guitar sides.

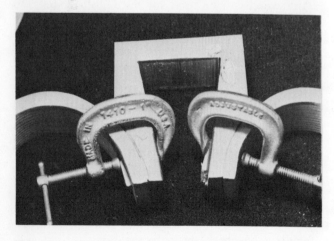

Fig. 115 Gluing the dovetail block to cut-aways.

Glue the sides and tailblock together, then glue to the cutaways. Glue this assembly to the dovetail block.

A multitude of blocks are shown for the lining strips. This unconventional approach is used to produce an arched top resembling a bell-shaped curve on the finished guitar. Lining strips are traditionally used to provide a wider gluing edge between the plates and the sides. As for clamping, the Martin Company has found that despite special clamps, they prefer clothes-pins. Use P.R.G. to glue, and when dry, sand linings smooth.

Place this unit on the plywood for the plates, and draw out the shape for the top and back. Turn unit over and check symmetry. Draw out the patterns of the "F" holes, drill a hole at each end and use a coping saw to cut out shape. Trim with files and sandpaper. Notice the wood is flat. The arch of this guitar is produced by a block that is glued inside the body, which produces a hump. Any wood can be used in making this block which will be glued under the space where the bridge will be. Position the block and glue the plates to the sides using an inch wide strip of wood the shape of the guitar to equalize pressure while clamping.

Use a router to cut a groove around the top and bottom of the guitar for gluing binding strips. You will need a one-point router guide to follow

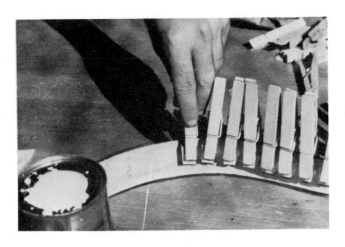

Fig. 116 Gluing the side linings.

Fig. 118 Outline of guitar drawn on wood for top and back.

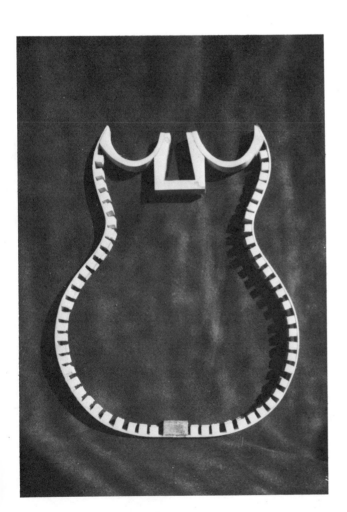

Fig. 117 The glued tailblock, sides, dovetail block, cut-aways and linings.

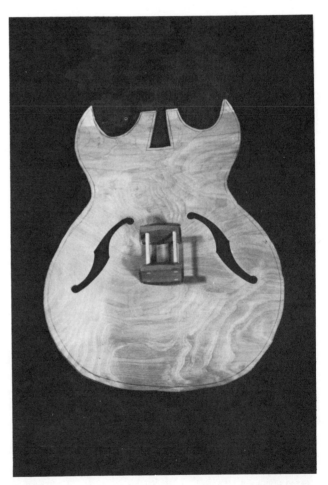

Fig. 119   The top cut out, with "F" holes and arch block.

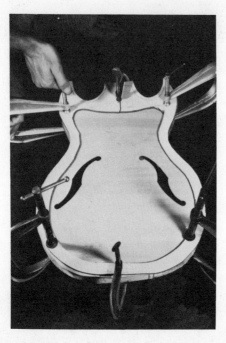

Fig. 121   Router with one touch point guide.

Fig. 120   Gluing on the top and back.

Fig. 122   Routing channel for body binding.

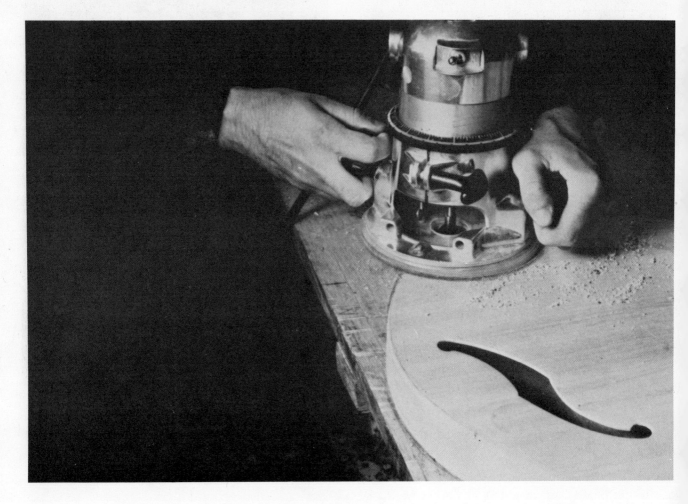

the curves of the body. Glue plastic binding with Duco cement. You will need a board shaped like the guitar with nails attached for rubber bands to hook onto. Put padding under the body before applying the band clamps.

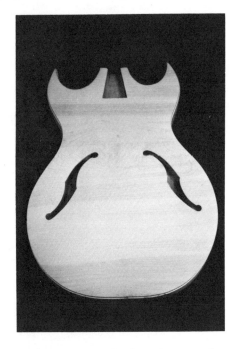

Fig. 123   The body after routing.

Fig. 124   Gluing the binding.

After the binding is completed, glue the neck to the body. Make sure the neck is straight and level. If you cut a loose dovetail, add wood shims. Now (or later) add small pieces of wood to fill the indentations of the dovetail so the neck is flush to the fretboard edge over the soundboard. Glue on the fretboard. Shape a nut and glue on. Use

Fig. 125   The body with the neck glued in place.

thread running down the 1st and 6th string notches to lay out placement of the tailpiece and pick-ups.

Drill holes for the controls and output jack. Drill holes in the area where the pick-up will go, connect with a small saw, and finish with files. Trial fit the controls by pulling them through the body with an attached thread. Use the same method for the output. Fasten the pick-ups. Now remove all parts and wire as shown in Tone and Volume controls chapter. Install the output first, then the controls, then the pick-up.

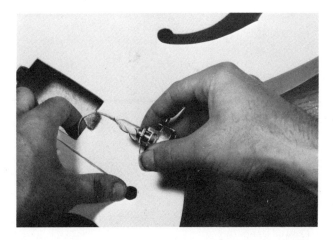

Fig. 126 The trick to installing pots inside the body.

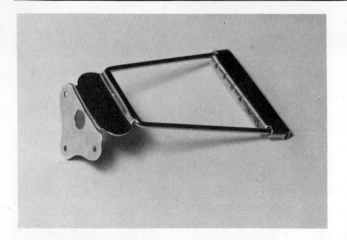

Fig. 127 The tailpiece.

Fig. 128 Half the building of the bridge.

Shown is a very inexpensive tailpiece. It is attached with three screws.

The bridge can be easily made from three or four pieces of wood that are glued together in a staggered fashion producing a channel to accept a saddle that is curved to conform to the fretboard arch. This can be rough sawn on a bandsaw and sanded to the finished shape.

Follow the chapter on finishing after the hardware is removed. This guitar was sprayed gloss white. The binding was scraped to show a black accent. The guitar's final coat was a clear lacquer.

Re-install hardware, install strings, and position the bridge. To find the exact position, sound a harmonic at the 12th fret and then press the string

Fig. 129 The completed bridge.

Fig. 130 Using a scraper to trim finish off binding.

down at the 12th fret and pluck. When the tones
match, the bridge is in the correct spot. I made a
wide saddle that allows for some string compensation length adjustment. Now plug in and enjoy
your guitar.

Fig. 131 The author and finished guitar.

The carving of an arched top and back guitar is complicated, but it can be done by hand if you have patience, and very sharp chisels. One method for this is to draw out cross section profiles of the plate corresponding to a grid of lines, say, $\frac{1}{2}$ inch apart. With these drawings plotting out the curves, you can measure the distances of the wood to be carved away. Holes can be drilled to be used as depth guides when carving. Many arched tops are about $\frac{1}{4}$ inch thick in the center going down to $\frac{1}{8}$ inch or less around the outside edges. For stability, it is best to carve the inside first and then the outside. The most common bracing is two parallel bars running down the length of the top, though sometimes tops and backs have no bracing. Often backs have bracing like a flat-top guitar back.

To efficiently produce arched guitars, large companies use a variety of automated equipment. The Gibson Company uses what could be compared to a radial arm saw/milling machine. Dado saw blades are linked to a guide that traces the finished shape in full length strokes. The guided blades cut a duplicate shape in the block to be shaped. Fender used to use a router, moved by hand, that was guided by a linked follower tracing across a finished shape. This type of device is often called a pantograph.

Fig. 132 Bracing on a typical arched-top.

Fig. 133 Holes drilled as a guide for carving an arched top or back.

A Guitar's Fretboard

MOST INSTRUMENT makers really do not enjoy hand cutting frets. The amateur builder is hard put to afford commercial fret-cutting machines that cut all the frets at once to the proper depth. I know several independent makers that have ground down a table saw blade to .025 in., bought carbide-tipped blades of .026 in. for $120., and some have made fret-cutting machines that resemble small radial arm saws using 3 in. .024-.030 machinist blades.

At the end of this chapter are lists of fret spacings given to me by John Hall of Rickenbacker. The basic fret formula is to divide the string length by 17.85, take the remaining distance and divide that, and so forth. The closer the frets move, the more critical the placement.

Though it has been stated that a fretboard should be level it actually needs a very slight curve along its length. If a string is fretted at the first and 20th fret, there should be a gap of .005 to .020 inch between the string and the 9th fret. This allows space for the shallow arc made by a vibrating string, and is necessary for the closest action possible. A 100% straight fretboard would have to have the strings higher above the frets to prevent a string from buzzing on the frets following where it was fingered.

The fretboard should be of hardwood because of wear on it. Pale wood would need to be sealed against soiling. The arched top of a fretboard facilitates fast playing. Most steel strung guitars have arched boards, classicals have flat boards because they are fingered differently.

Any very hard wood that can be glued could be used for a fretboard. The standard is Gaboon ebony from Africa. I use Macassar ebony from the Far East. It has streaks of black and brown and is considerably cheaper than African wood, while its hardness is similar.

Plane the wood to a 1/4 in. thickness. Cut out the tapered shape. Use files and sandpaper to arch the board. I find it easy to make a fretboard flat by sanding it with sandpaper rubber cemented to a carpenter's level.

Fig. 134 Miter box for cutting frets. The slotted blocks guide the blade and allow only a certain depth of cut.

Draw a center line down the fretboard. Measure out the fret spacing along this line. Using a "T"-shaped guide you can make for yourself, scribe a perpendicular line at each of the positions for a fret. You can cut fret notches now. A center line drawn down the mitre box helps alignment.

Some form of position markers, such as mother of pearl dots, are commonly inlaid in fretbards. The usual locations are in the space just before the 5th, 7th, 9th, 12th & 15th frets. The Stuart McDonald Co. catalog shows how to do more complex inlay projects and advertises the necessary equipment. For simple mother of pearl dots, drill the holes and glue in with Duco cement. Finish sanding the board to trim everything up, end with 600 grit sandpaper. Apply furniture polishing oil such as Watco. Completely black African ebony is a favored material to inlay into, because it is easy to fill in small gaps during inlaying with black filler. Since the wood is uniformly black, it is easy to match. The black colour makes a pleasant background for the shimmering pearl.

Fret wire is "T"-shaped wire. The bottom of the T is hammered into a notch for a non-glued, pressed fit. Gluing makes refretting difficult. Low frets are easier to use in regard to finger pressure applied when played, but wear out quicker. The narrower the top of the T the more precise the positions of string stopping will be, but here again less metal, less lifetime.

Use wire-cutters to cut wire to the length needed. Bending frets before fitting makes the fit to the arch easier to achieve. Use a file to trim the overhang close to the edge. Slide the fretboard's edge against a large perfectly flat board covered with sandpaper to do final trimming, producing a flat edge. The edge can be bound now if you care to. Binding serves to make a smooth decorative edge. Remember that binding increases the width. If you're going the bound route, make the wood narrower. Use a sharp knife and sandpaper to scrape and sand the binding to its finished shape.

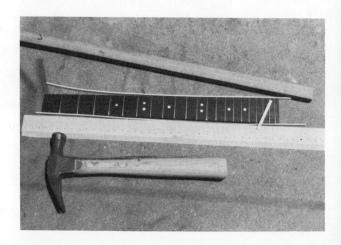

Fig. 135 Hinged clamp for gluing fretboard binding.

Fig. 136 Hammering in frets.

Fig. 137 Sanding fret edges flush on flat board covered with coarse and fine sandpaper.

An alternative method is to proceed through notching and inlaying, and then glue the board on the neck. Now it is sanded level and the frets installed. This way a level fretboard is assured. It is very hard to make a bound fretboard this way however. The sharp edge of frets can be smoothed with hand held emery paper slid along the edge.

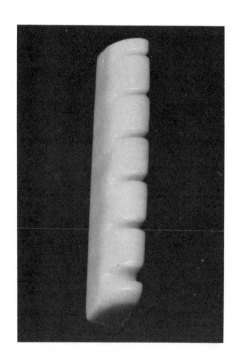

Fig. 139 The string nut is the same for both guitars.

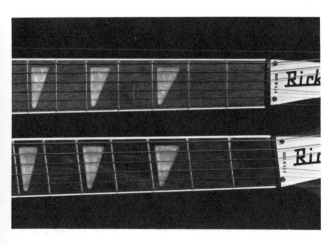

Fig. 138 Straight and slanted Rickenbacker frets.

These fret spacings were provided by the Rickenbacker Company. I encourage builders to make guitars with 24 fret (two octave) necks like so many guitar companies finally do.

These fret spacings are the result of a sophisticated computer print-out. The basic fret formula given on page 77 needs additional tempering after the fret placement is calculated. This is to compensate for changing tension at the different positions a string is fretted. The following print-out does not need compensation.

© Rickenbacker 1974, used by permission.

Scale Length = 24 inches		Scale Length = 24.25 inches		Scale Length = 24.50 inches	
Fret No.	Length from Nut	Fret No.	Length from Nut	Fret No.	Length from Nut
1	1.347	1	1.361	1	1.375
2	2.618	2	2.645	2	2.672
3	3.818	3	3.858	3	3.898
4	4.951	4	5.002	4	5.054
5	6.020	5	6.083	5	6.145
6	7.029	6	7.102	6	7.175
7	7.981	7	8.065	7	8.148
8	8.880	8	8.973	8	9.065
9	9.729	9	9.830	9	9.932
10	10.530	10	10.640	10	10.749
11	11.286	11	11.404	11	11.521
12	12.000	12	12.125	12	12.250
13	12.673	13	12.805	13	12.937
14	13.309	14	13.447	14	13.586
15	13.909	15	14.054	15	14.199
16	14.475	16	14.626	16	14.777
17	15.010	17	15.166	17	15.322
18	15.514	18	15.676	18	15.837
19	15.990	19	16.157	19	16.324
20	16.440	20	16.611	20	16.782
21	16.864	21	17.040	21	17.216
22	17.265	22	17.445	22	17.624
23	17.643	23	17.827	23	18.010
24	18.000	24	18.187	24	18.375
25	18.336	25	18.527	25	18.718

Scale Length = 24.75 inches

Fret No.	Length from Nut
1	1.389
2	2.700
3	3.937
4	5.105
5	6.208
6	7.249
7	8.231
8	9.158
9	10.033
10	10.859
11	11.639
12	12.375
13	13.069
14	13.725
15	14.343
16	14.927
17	15.479
18	15.999
19	16.490
20	16.954
21	17.391
22	17.804
23	18.194
24	18.562
25	18.909

Scale Length = 25.25 inches

Fret No.	Length from Nut
1	1.417
2	2.754
3	4.017
4	5.209
5	6.333
6	7.395
7	8.397
8	9.343
9	10.236
10	11.078
11	11.874
12	12.625
13	13.333
14	14.002
15	14.633
16	15.229
17	15.791
18	16.322
19	16.823
20	17.296
21	17.743
22	18.164
23	18.562
24	18.937
25	19.291

Scale Length = 25.75 inches

Fret No.	Length from Nut
1	1.445
2	2.809
3	4.096
4	5.312
5	6.459
6	7.542
7	8.563
8	9.528
9	10.438
10	11.298
11	12.109
12	12.875
13	13.597
14	14.279
15	14.923
16	15.531
17	16.104
18	16.646
19	17.156
20	17.639
21	18.094
22	18.524
23	18.929
24	19.312
25	19.673

Scale Length = 25 inches

Fret No.	Length from Nut
1	1.403
2	2.727
3	3.977
4	5.157
5	6.271
6	7.322
7	8.314
8	9.250
9	10.134
10	10.969
11	11.756
12	12.500
13	13.201
14	13.863
15	14.488
16	15.078
17	15.635
18	16.161
19	16.657
20	17.125
21	17.567
22	17.984
23	18.378
24	18.750
25	19.100

Scale Length = 25.50 inches

Fret No.	Length from Nut
1	1.431
2	2.782
3	4.057
4	5.260
5	6.396
6	7.468
7	8.480
8	9.436
9	10.337
10	11.188
11	11.991
12	12.750
13	13.465
14	14.141
15	14.778
16	15.380
17	15.948
18	16.484
19	16.990
20	17.468
21	17.918
22	18.344
23	18.745
24	19.125
25	19.482

Scale Length = 26 inches

Fret No.	Length from Nut
1	1.459
2	2.836
3	4.136
4	5.363
5	6.522
6	7.615
7	8.647
8	9.621
9	10.540
10	11.407
11	12.226
12	13.000
13	13.729
14	14.418
15	15.068
16	15.681
17	16.261
18	16.807
19	17.323
20	17.810
21	18.270
22	18.703
23	19.113
24	19.500
25	19.864

Wiring Circuits

THE TONE and volume control on most common electric guitars are potentiometers (pots). Pots are variable resistors. Resistance to current is regulated by turning the knob on the shaft of the pot. When the shaft is turned, an arm inside the resistor moves along a path of a gradually changing resistance contact wall. A single pot on a line will limit the current, serving as a volume control. The speed control of a sewing machine foot pedal is a variable resistor.

In order to make a pot behave as a tone control, a capacitor is wired in series with it, with one capacitor lead wired to a ground point. High frequency signals will pass through the capacitor toward the ground. The pot regulates the amount of high frequencies that are allowed to pass. The higher the value of the capacitor, the greater the treble cut.

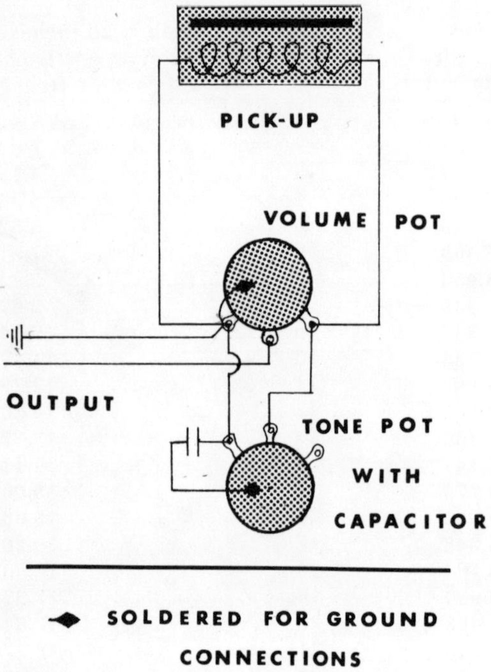

Fig. 141   Two Clarostat pots, one with knob.

Now what should the values be of the pots and the capacitor? This depends on the output of the pick-ups and the scope of the treble cut desired.

Pots come with either audio or linear taper. The linear has uniform, progressive action; audio taper has a slower take off but allows adjustment at high levels with more delicate operation than linear taper. Audio taper is made to conform to characteristics of the ear. Some people, however, prefer the linear.

Telecaster model guitars use audio taper 250 K Ohm pots and .02 micro-farad capacitor. 500 K pots and .05 U capacitors are commonly used on other guitars. Many builders experiment with these values to get the sound they want. If the value is too low on the pot, however, it impedes the voltage input.

Varitone tone controls are a very simple solution to achieve more variety of tone than you can with one capacitor. The Varitone uses five capacitors of different values wired to a selector switch. With this arrangement, different values can be selected to go along with the tone pot.

Now it should be understood that I have not explained micro-farads, or K Ohms: I cannot give

PICK-UP

VOLUME POT

OUTPUT

TONE POT

WITH

CAPACITOR

◆━ **SOLDERED FOR GROUND CONNECTIONS**

Fig. 140 A simple two pot volume and tone control circuit for an electric guitar. Two such circuits are used in the solid-body guitar.

a course on electronics in this chapter. Without knowledge of electronics, it is better to switch around values to see what happens, if you do stick close to the values spoken of above. Many trained guitar builders experiment by trial and error to find a tone capacitor value that gives a sound they prefer.

Pots have limitations as to how they cut-off current. There can be greater control of tone if more elaborate circuits are used. High and low pass filters and chokes, which are constructed with the use of semiconductors, are a possible solution.

As stated above, a capacitor passes high frequencies more easily than lower ones. An inductance, or choke coil, passes lower frequencies more readily than higher ones. This can also happen in a pickup coil. An incredibly bulky system could be made with coils, capacitors, resistors and tubes. Thanks to aero-space technology, we now have integrated circuits. Transistors work like miniature tubes and I.C.'s are miniature transistor, diode and resistor networks. The I.C.'s shown in the Alembic guitar are very common systems. In the guitar field, finding persons who know how to use them is far from common. Electric organ companies have done a vast amount of work making circuits that filter out selected frequencies and boost selected harmonics. Sustain, decay and echo can all be modulated.

If you want a challenging project, design a circuit that will produce the quality of sound by an acoustic guitar at rock concert levels with no feed back. If you can do this, musicians will make you rich and famous.

Fig. 142 A four-pole five-throw switch.

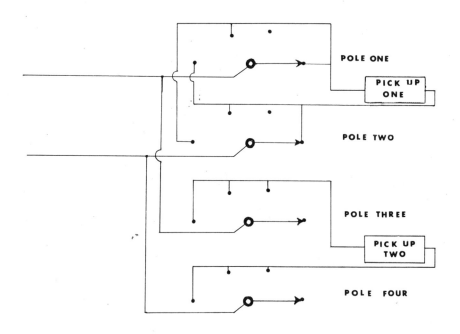

Fig. 143 Diagram of wiring for a four-pole four-throw rotary switch.

On page 83 is a plan of a four-pole four-position selector switch. The switch shown is a Centralab PA-1013 four-pole, five-position unit. There are tabs that are adjusted for the number of positions wanted. There are two poles on each deck of the switch. Basic instructions come with the switch. This circuit provides positions:

1. Pick-up #1 only.
2. Pick-up #2 only.
3. Both pick-ups in phase
4. Both pick-ups out of phase.

This is the volume tone circuit used on the hollow body. Two such circuits are used on the solid body of this book.

Note that the volume and tone controls are not shown, for better clarity when switching between diagrams. The grounded output goes to the output jack to connect with the plug's cup-like terminal. The live lead is wired to connect to the tip of the plug.

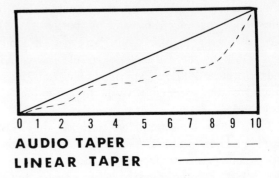

AUDIO TAPER ─ ─ ─ ─ ─ ─ ─
LINEAR TAPER ─────────

Fig. 144 Diagram of different rates of change between audio and linear taper pots.

Fig. 145 The circuit board tone controls inside an Alembic guitar.

Finishing

THE ELECTRIC GUITAR is probably the exact opposite, in regard to finishing, as the violin. The finishing of a violin is a very important factor of sound quality. The electric guitar's is mainly to protect against wear and tear and add decoration.

When painting or staining wood, any scratches are emphasized. It is important to have the wood perfectly smooth. When using stain, scratches catch more stain than the surrounding areas and will stand out. A gloss finish also points out scratches.

After the guitar is sanded to a scratch-free surface, first stain and oil it for a natural matte style finish; or instead, use a sealer compatable to the colour and clear protective coats you'll apply. A third alternative would be to stain and then use a glossy clear finish. Since the finish has virtually no effect on sound, anything from flat one-color paints to metallic or metalflake paints can be used. Custom-made car paint jobs give ideas of what can be done. Check out hot rod magazines.

The guitars in this book have solid color glossy finishes. The wood was sealed with clear lacquer, then sanded smooth and coloured, spray-lacquer paint applied. The final coat was a glossy clear lacquer. The finish was sanded between coats and polished with powered rottenstone and then silicon/wax auto polish.

THE SUNBURST finish probably started as an imitation of old violins. The simplest sunburst is no more than a dark coloured paint sprayed around a guitar at some distance to produce a blended finish. Better sunbursts are a progression of colour, yellow in the center, blending to orange, red and then dark brown. Sunbursts are done fairly easily with an airbrush. The best ones are not sprayed, but rather a progression of overlapping rubbed-on stains. A final clear finish is then put over this. Prevention of scratches and stains is even more important in this case.

Sunburst finishes can be done in various colour ranges—reds, blues, greens, purples, etc. Use your imagination—and good luck.

OIL FINISHING, as mentioned earlier, is preferred by some people. Using a high quality oil-resin, a matte protective surface is produced. Its advantages are that it doesn't show wear as badly as a polished gloss. It doesn't peel or scratch off.

Basically all that is done is to apply a liberal amount of finishing oil, let it soak in, and then buff the surface. Use oil meant for furniture; other oils may not dry and/or will turn rancid and smell.

Fig. 146 The body being suspended while being sprayed.

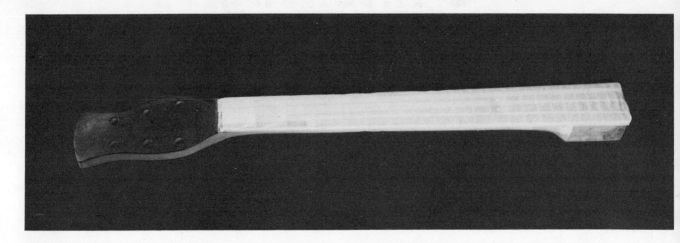

Fig. 147 The neck with fretboard masked just before having finish applied.

Fig. 148 The body being polished.

Materials And Suppliers

YOU SHOULD, ideally, have a whole wood-shop available. Perhaps there's an adult wood-shop class near you to take adavantage of. The tools that you will need are a band saw (a bow saw or coping saw could be used in substitution), a table saw/hand saw, chisels, power planer, hand planes, drill press/hand drill and jig, router carving chisels, spokeshave, rasps, screwdriver, soldering iron, fret saw, sanding block, cabinet and C clamps. It is possible to figure out how to make clamping jigs that apply pressure with sliding wedges if you do not have metal clamps.

MATERIALS FOR A SOLID BODY GUITAR

WOOD—maple suggested.

BODY—Center: 1 piece 1¾ x 2⅛ x 16½ (in.)

BODY—Right side: 1 piece 1¾ x 5½ x 17

BODY—Left side: 1 piece 1¾ x 5½ x 18½

NECK: 2 pieces 1¾ x 1½ x 26

FRETBOARD—ebony, rosewood or maple. One piece ¼ x 2½ x 18⅛ inches

Head veneer: 1 piece 1/16 x 3 x 6½

Mechanical and Electrical Parts:

One humbucking pick-up of any kind

One telecaster lead pick-up

Two 5/16 in. square mild steel rods 19 inches long

Four 250 or 500 K Ohm Pots, Clarostat or Omar Bradley recommended. Knob type is optional.

One four-pole four-position switch.

Two .05 micro-farad capacitors, mylar dip. Preferably under 100 volts and over 10 volts.

One output jack.

Insulated connection wire. Shielded twin lead wire is recommended.

One piece of pickguard material 11 x 15 in.

One Stratocaster bridge

One set of tuning machines with vertical posts.

One ivory, bone or plastic nut.

Glue, strings, paint, finishing materials, four feet of fret wire and fret position dots.

MATERIALS FOR A HOLLOW BODY GUITAR

BODY—top and back: 2 pieces ⅛ x 15 x 20 (inches) hardwood plywood

BODY—sides: 2 pieces ⅛ x 1½ x 23 hardwood

NECK: 2 pieces 1¾ x 1½ x 26

Fretboard: Same as for solid body.

DOVETAIL BLOCK—1½ x 3½ x 3½ hard-

Any kind of wood ½ x ½ in. in length cut to make linings.

HEAD VENEER: 1 piece 1/16 x 3 x 6½

Wood for bridge equivalent to 1 piece ½ x ¾ x 5 hardwood

Wood to make an arch block as shown in plans, any configuration that works would do.

Mechanical and Electrical Parts

One magnetic pick-up

Two pots 250 or 500 K Ohm and knobs

One .05 micro-farad capacitor for tone control

Insulated connection wire

One output jack

One adjustable truss rod made from two 18 in. lengths of 3/16 in. fine thread steel rod, a truss rod nut and washer

One set of tuning machines with vertical posts.

One ivory, bone or plastic nut.

Glue, strings, four feet fret wire, fret position dots, paint/finishing materials and ten feet of plastic binding.

The tailpiece.

WHERE TO BUY MATERIALS

For pick-ups, pots, and related components I recommend your local music store. The Alembic Co. (60 Brady St.) in San Francisco handles the best electronic parts for electric guitars if you're so inclined by talent and financial situation.

If you are doing advanced magnet construction, The Permag Corp. (with many locations) manufactures industrial magnets. They carry many types of Alnico ceramic and rare earth magnets! Electronic supply houses sell magnet wire.

For inlay and binding materials I recommend Stewart-McDonald Co., Box 900 Athens, Ohio; and Erika Banjos, Van Nuys, California.

For amps, sound support equipment, and related information I recommend Warehouse Sound, Railroad Square, San Luis Obispo, California.

For woodworking tools, Woodcraft Supply, 8 Henshaw St., Woburn, Mass. 01801 carries the best made.

For Wood, if you cannot find it locally—White Brothers Lumber, 4801 Tidewater, Oakland, Ca., will supply wood sufficient for either/or both a solid body and a hollow body guitar if there is sufficient demand.

Kit #2 will be a choice of a mahogany or maple solid body.

Kit #3 will be for a hollow body with mahogany neck and hardwood plywood top and back.

Additional guitar wood and equipment suppliers are:

Guitar Center, P.O. Box 15444, Tulsa, Okla. 74115

Vitali Import Co., 5944 Atlantic Blvd., Los Angeles, Ca. 90270

Guitars Unlimited Sales, P.O. Box 11449, Fort Worth, Texas 76109 (Guitars and guitar hardware and electronics)

Allied Traders, P.O. Box 603, Kendall Branch Miami, Fla. 33156 (Guitar building supplies)

Musicians Supply, Inc., P.O. Box 4507, San Diego, Ca. 92104 (Guitar hardware and electronics)

J.F. Wallo, 1319 F St. N.W., Washington, D.C. (Guitar building suplies)

Glossary

Action: How close the strings are to the fretboard and how straight that fretboard is. Fast action occurs with light gauge strings close to a perfectly flat fretboard. High or stiff action occurs when heavy gauge strings are high above the frets. When a string is pressed down at the first and 12th frets, the maximum allowable space between the string and the sixth fret is about .015 in.

Arch-Top: The top of an instrument that is a compound curve, like an upside down shallow bowl. A violin has an arched top and back. The finest arched tops are not bent, but rather carved from one large block of wood. Bending and pressure forming induces stresses which hamper the sound producing vibrations.

Binding: Thin strips of wood or plastic around a guitar body. It seals end grain against moisture changes, provides a protective edge and is ornamental.

Bridge: The device used for stopping the sounding length of the strings opposite the tuning machines and nut.

Courses: A 12-string guitar is a 6-course instrument. Courses are strings that are fingered as though they were one.

Distortion: Inaccurate sound reproduction. What most people mean by electric guitar distortion is overdriving an amp to produce a sound that is fuzzy. It's easy to blow an amp if you don't know what you're doing. Overdriving means giving the amp a signal too strong for it to handle.

"F" Holes: Sound holes on a hollow body in the shape of an italic ' *f* '. This is what violins have.

Feedback: When a sound system amplifies its own output, like a microphone or guitar used in front of its own speaker. Jimi Hendrix knew how to control it and use it as an element of his music.

Fingerboard: A piece of hardwood over which the strings pass and can be stopped to various lengths to produce various notes. For correct usage the term should be used for instruments such as a violin. A guitar has frets along its finger board, and this is called a fretboard.

Flat-top: A guitar that has a sound board that is flat, i.e., not arched—like an ordinary country/folk guitar, a Martin D-28.

Fretless: Not having frets, like a violin.

Frets: Strips of wire placed at precise spots across a fingerboard to produce a specific scale. Very old instruments had pieces of gut tied to the neck to act as frets. Old steel string guitars had thin slices of metal inserted in the fretboard that were trimmed to a desired height. Frets are now made of "T" cross-section-shaped wire. The bottom of the "T" is inserted in a notch cut into the fretboard.

Hawaiian Guitar: The first such instruments were ordinary guitars with high action to facilitate playing with a slide instead of fingering. Later Hawaiian guitars lost the Spanish guitar body and were basically a beam of metal or wood with strings across it that were electrically amplified. The pedal steel is a descendant of the Hawaiian guitar.

Hollow-body: A guitar with a hollow-body that is used to shape its sound.

Intonation: A note sounding the precise frequency it is supposed to sound.

Nut: The stopping point of the sounding length of the strings near the tuning machines, at the end opposite the bridge.

Pedal Steel: An instrument of usually ten strings that run horizontal and is played with a slide. Foot pedals are used to change keys and produce sound effects.

Phasing: The relationship of the negative and positive leads of, especially, pick-ups. "In phase" occurs when two pick-ups are both hooked up in the same way. "Out-of-phase" occurs when they are opposite. Different changes in sound are produced by being in phase, out-of-phase and switching back and forth between the two.

Pick-up: A device used to pick-up vibration-caused signals and send them to an amplifier. A pick-up uses a very small electrical current and it's also called a transducer.

Plate: A top or back.

Position Markers: Inlays on the fretboard for decoration which also make it easier to differentiate frets.

Pots (Potentiometer): Device for controlling current in a circuit.. Volume and tone controls are pots. A variable resistor.

Purfling: Strips of binding inlaid around a guitar to seal against moisture and provide decoration. Very complex binding is called Purfling on guitars. Traditional Purfling is strips inlaid a distance in from the edge. A violin has Purfling.

Response: The resultant sound of a guitar or amp to tones being played.

Ribs: The curved sides of a hollow body guitar.

Roundhole: A guitar with a round soundhole, usually with a flat top.

Slide Guitar: Hawaiian guitar—a guitar that has the strings stopped, not by the fingers on the frets, rather has a sliding piece of metal, glass or plastic on the strings.

Solid Body: An electric guitar made of solid material—not hollow. Most common are wood, though aluminum, plastic and stone have been used.

Soundboard: The main sound-producing element on an acoustic guitar—the top.

Sound hole: A hole(s) on the soundboard of an acoustic guitar where sound is emitted.

Steel Guitar: Hawaiian guitar.

Stereo (guitar): An electric with two pick-ups, each of which is one channel on a stereo amp, or a pick-up split to provide two channels.

Sustain: The length of time a tone lasts after a string is plucked.

Tailpiece: The lower mounting point of strings mainly on arch-topped guitars.

Tuning Machines: Geared twisting levers used for tightening strings to desired pitch.

Bibliography

Cady, W. G. *Piezoelectricity.* New York: McGraw Hill, 1946.

Clifford, Martin, *Basic Electricity and Beginning Electronics.* Blue Ridge Summit, Pa.: Tab Books, 1973.

Dorf, Richard H. *Electronic Musical Instruments.* New York: Radio File, 1968.

Douglas, Alan and Astley S. *Transistor Electronic Organs for the Amateur.* London, U.K.: Sir Isaac Pitman and Sons, 1965.

Hibbs, Nelsen, *Basic Electronic Circuits Simplified.* Blue Ridge Summit, Pa.: Tab Books, 1972.

Schematics

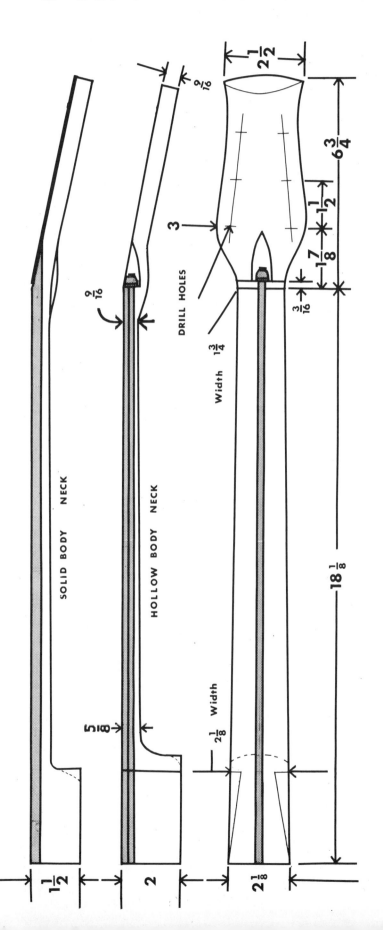

SOLID BODY NECK

HOLLOW BODY NECK

$1\frac{1}{2}$

2

$2\frac{1}{8}$

$\frac{9}{16}$

$\frac{9}{16}$

$\frac{5}{8}$

$2\frac{1}{8}$ Width

$2\frac{1}{2}$

$6\frac{3}{4}$

$1\frac{1}{2}$

$1\frac{7}{8}$

3

DRILL HOLES

Width $1\frac{3}{4}$

$\frac{3}{16}$

$18\frac{1}{8}$

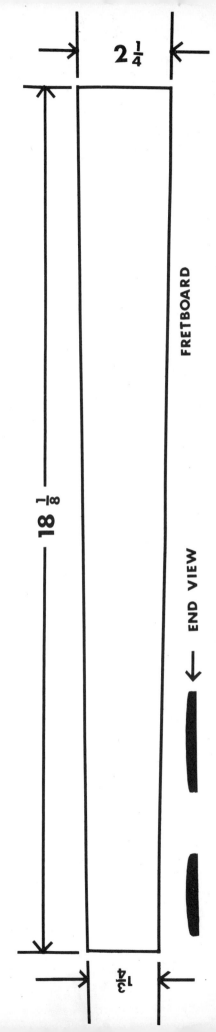

$2\frac{1}{4}$

FRETBOARD

$18\frac{1}{8}$

$\frac{3}{4}$

END VIEW

To make a pattern for the guitar bodies, place a piece of $1/2$ in. grid rule tracing paper over the plans in the book. On a sheet of paper with 1 in. grid pattern, plot out the shape of the guitar square by square. This will give you a full size pattern. The shaded areas are where the body can be shaped to better fit the player. The Stratocaster embodies this feature.

$2\frac{1}{8}$

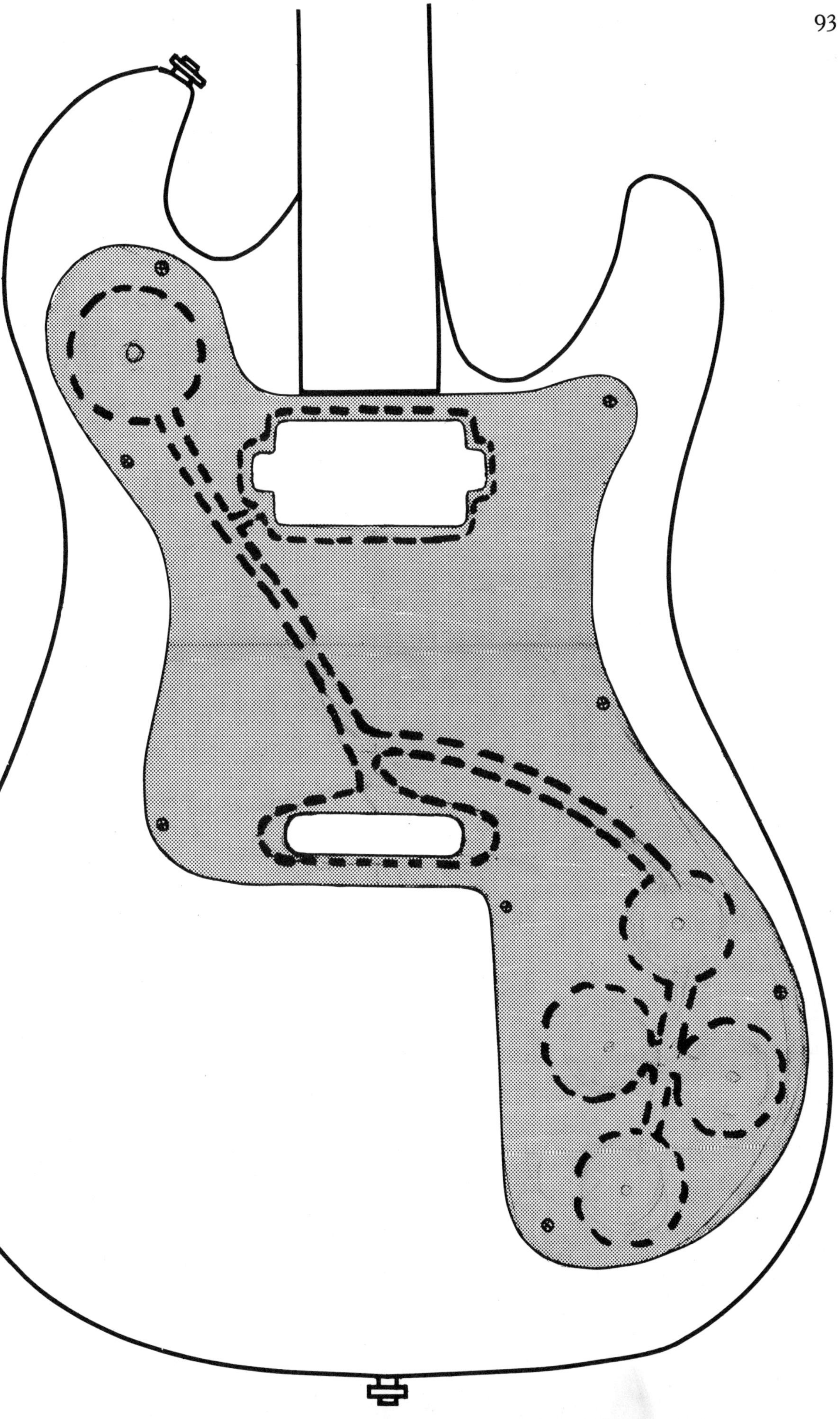

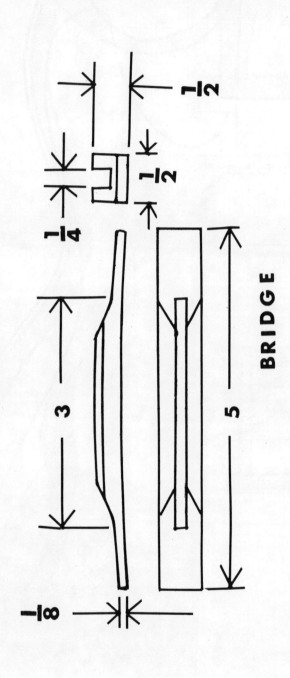

BRIDGE

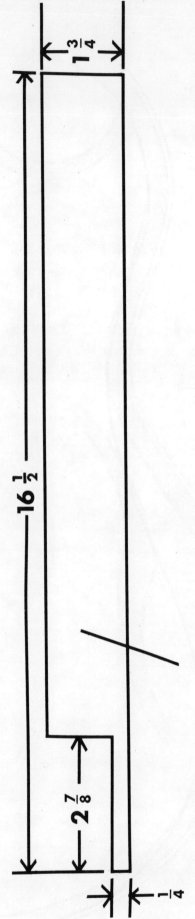

BODY—Center

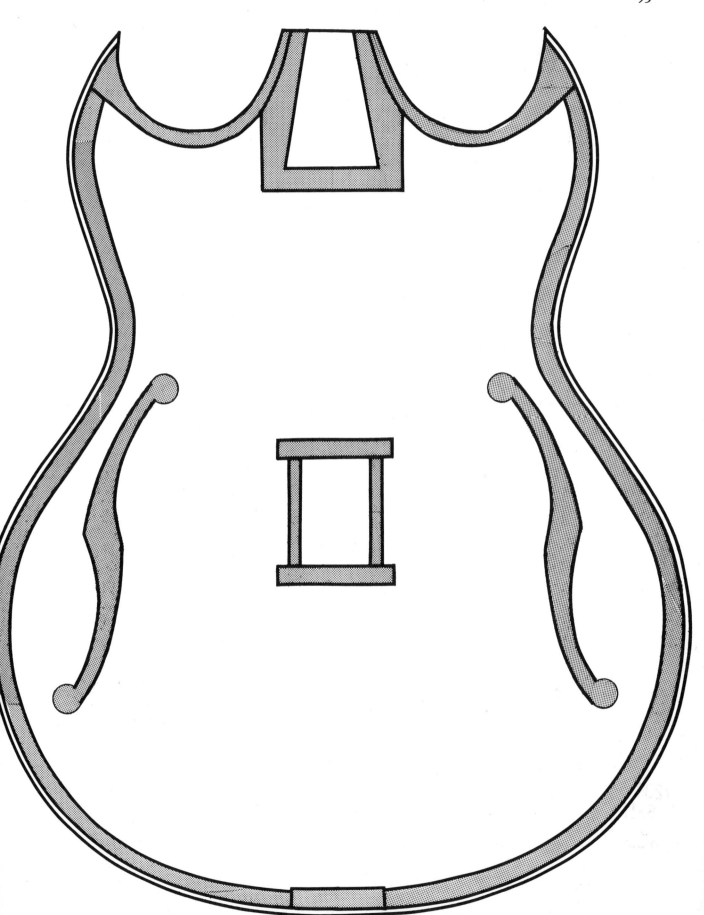

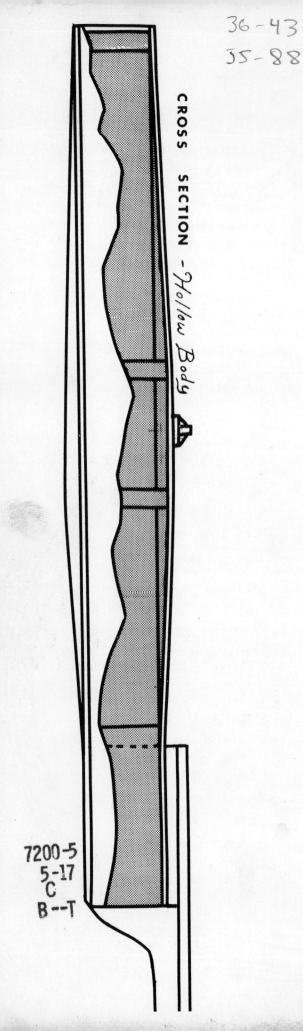

CROSS SECTION – *Hollow Body*

36-43
55-88

7200-5
5-17
C
B--T

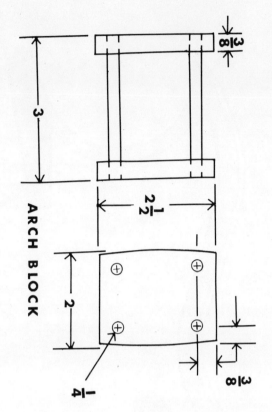

ARCH BLOCK

$\frac{3}{8}$

3

$2\frac{1}{2}$

2

$\frac{1}{4}$

$\frac{3}{8}$

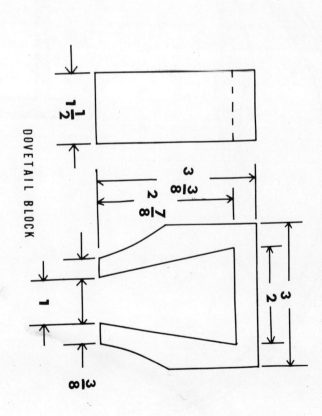

DOVETAIL BLOCK

$1\frac{1}{2}$

$3\frac{3}{8}$

$2\frac{7}{8}$

$2\frac{3}{3}$

1

$\frac{3}{8}$